D

're are to be ret

20TH-CENTURY COMPOSERS

Leonard Bernstein

Leonard Bernstein

by Paul Myers

Φ

Phaidon Press Limited
Regent's Wharf
All Saints Street
London N1 9PA

First published 1998
Reprinted 1998
© 1998 Phaidon Press Limited

ISBN 0 7148 3701 6

A CIP catalogue record for this book is
available from the British Library.

Library of Congress Cataloging in
Publication Data available.

Printed in Singapore

Frontispiece, the composer at
the piano, Warsaw, 1959

Contents

Introduction

A few days after Leonard Bernstein's death, I was in the office of a
well-known middle-European conductor, a man seldom generous
when assessing his colleagues. 'Bernstein?' he shrugged dismissively.
'He was always such an exhibitionist; a playboy.' He smiled unkindly.
'I suppose it's rather sad – a little like when the great clown Grock
died!' His young American assistant stared at him in disbelief. 'How
can you say that? You're talking about one of the greatest musicians of
our time. He brought the classics to millions of people who'd never
thought of listening to them, and he inspired thousands of musicians
and students: kids like me, maybe two or three generations of us. My
God, it was because of Lenny that I became a conductor!'

Both reactions were typical of the contradictory emotions that
Leonard Bernstein inspired. You either loved him or hated him;
nothing much in between. His critics were almost as numerous as his
admirers, and he seldom found favour with the conservative musical
hierarchy; that said, to the general public and to those aspiring
musicians he encouraged, Bernstein personified the romance, the
drama, the passion and, in his own words, the joy of music.

Despite a multiplicity of talents, any one of which would have
made him a leading figure among his peers, Bernstein considered
himself to be primarily a composer. Considering that he was one of
the busiest conductors of his generation, torn between international
concert appearances and finding adequate isolation and time to write,
his creative output was surprisingly large and varied, producing as
much music as many full-time composers of the same era.

The international acclaim given to his Broadway ventures,
particularly *West Side Story*, haunted him in later years and he feared
that he would be remembered only for them. To have been
responsible for one of the finest musicals in the history of the theatre
would satisfy most creative ambitions, but Bernstein's rejection of such
an image is understandable. He was a classically trained, highly
educated musician and, as one of the world's leading conductors,

he knew and had performed virtually all of the great masterpieces. It was only natural that he wanted his 'serious' compositions to be worthy of joining the immortals. He sought recognition as the composer of three symphonies and numerous other orchestral works, the operas *A Quiet Place* and *Trouble in Tahiti*, three full-length ballets, many choral and vocal compositions, and various chamber and instrumental pieces.

As a person, he was a product of *The Age of Anxiety*, the poem by W. H. Auden that inspired his Second Symphony, and both his public and private lives reveal a series of contradictions that reflect the complexities and pressure of twentieth-century life. Almost a lifelong occupant of the psychiatrist's couch, frequently switching from one 'shrink' to the next, he was a complicated, sensitive yet flamboyant and passionately creative man of dazzling intellectual powers who lived in a perennial spotlight that he both loved and resented. In an endless tug-of-war between the desire for instant adulation on the concert podium and immortality through his compositions, he seemed to be driven by Jekyll and Hyde forces which he recognized in himself and which affected many aspects of his behaviour.

I first encountered Leonard Bernstein in 1962, when I was a newly employed producer at Columbia Records in New York, and we met quite frequently over the next eighteen years, particularly during the 1970s when I was stationed in Europe and Bernstein was establishing stronger ties in Vienna, Paris and London. In America I had attended many New York Philharmonic concerts and first witnessed his magnetic, almost hypnotic, power to command attention. Some performers – Danny Kaye and Feodor Chaliapin, for example – possess a charisma, a metaphysical 'presence', that sets them apart. So it was with Bernstein. When you watched him conduct, you were often convinced that you were witnessing the performance of a lifetime. Sometimes this was the case, but if you broke the hypnotic link with Bernstein by shutting your eyes or shifting your attention to follow the score, you would often become aware of many discrepancies: unexpected rhythmic changes, poor ensemble, exaggerated emphases and other musical effects not requested by the composer. But you were still in the presence of a supreme and convincing musical communicator (and how very few there have been *since* Bernstein!). This connection with the audience was one of the reasons – the others were more mundanely based on economics and the recording costs of orchestras – why he often preferred to record live concerts rather than make special studio tapings. He inspired his audiences, and they in turn inspired him.

Many aspects of Bernstein's life and career were influenced by his contradictory and contrary changes of mood. He could be brilliant, witty, charming and generous, particularly in promoting the work of fellow American composers. These qualities endeared him to an international public, and established an army of dedicated acolytes who served under him. But their hero also displayed enough human frailties to cause consternation among his most loyal supporters. In his excellent and superbly researched biography, Humphrey Burton – a friend and working colleague of Bernstein's for about thirty years – writes tolerantly of the man's *hubris*: originally, scorn of the gods, which brings about the nemesis or downfall of a hero. Others are less forgiving, noting only how the darker side of Bernstein's character tormented him throughout his life.

Much – probably too much – has been written already about his bisexuality, particularly its homosexual aspects, and while such material makes titillating gossip, it has little to do with composing music. But, just as his life was divided between composing and conducting, Bernstein's ambivalent sexuality was characteristically contradictory. At times, emulating his hero Koussevitzky, who believed that a conductor must keep himself 'pure' and 'clean', Bernstein was often contemptuously homophobic (which might have been a manifestation of the self-hatred that some of his biographers have suggested). On the other hand, he was promiscuously homosexual, despite being a loving husband and adoring father.

As a young man, his ambition had been boundless and he had been something of a whiz-kid: the central figure at every teenage party, dominating the room from the piano with anything from Bach to boogie-woogie. His determination to be the centre of attention never diminished, although it was tempered in time by his many successes. Even so, his egocentric behaviour often gave way to vanity and a selfish arrogance that were both unattractive and unnecessary.

The pianist Glenn Gould, a friend and admirer, once said, 'Lenny won't age well. He'll never let go of being Peter Pan.' That was in the mid 1960s, when Bernstein was about forty-six, but Gould's prophesy was sadly fulfilled. Latterly, there were many Bernstein triumphs but also a growing number of disappointing failures; once a handsome, athletically trim and elegantly fashionable maestro, the older Bernstein was overweight, pallidly unhealthy and often disshevelled. His face seemed to reveal, in each deeply lined crease, crow's foot and shadow, a lifetime of disappointment, self-indulgence and dissipation.

In his final decade, his dependence on alcohol and cigarettes, and his misuse of medicinal drugs, together with critical failures and the ageing process, clearly inhibited the strength and ardour of earlier times. He still drove himself at a frenetic pace, constantly demanded and adored by a worldwide public, and some of his interpretations on the concert platform were as magical as ever. But others were submerged beneath tasteless overstatement and patently wilful distortion. I was present at a London concert at which a performance of Elgar's *Enigma Variations* seemed to be stretched almost beyond recognition. But more embarrassing than the stage performance was the backstage arrogance with which Bernstein dismissed Elgar and the long line of British conductors who had interpreted his music. Usually Bernstein's charm, his ready wit and his sudden gestures of thoughtfulness or generosity were still there, but they too could be overshadowed by ugly displays of childish petulance, overriding vanity and foolish posturing, seemingly played to a gallery of sycophantic, self-serving hangers-on. Many erstwhile colleagues and admirers became tired of his obnoxious outbursts, finding that he had become a public liability and a private boor. (In earlier years, he was never misled by the hangers-on. In 1971, for example, he conducted performances of Strauss's *Der Rosenkavalier* in Vienna at the State Opera, prior to recording it. Although the dress rehearsal did not go well, he received the usual lavish congratulations. A young woman, however, who had been assigned by CBS to look after his publicity, visited him in his dressing-room afterwards and smiled consolingly, assuring him that a bad dress rehearsal was a good omen for the first night. At her words, Bernstein's face lit up, and he grasped her hands, saying, 'At last, someone who's prepared to tell me the truth!')

Over the years, my own association with Bernstein was somewhat eccentric. As I was the European representative of his record company (with which he was growing frustrated), Bernstein treated me in a friendly, always cordial but slightly distant manner. He usually travelled in company, surrounded by his business manager, personal assistant, record producer and any number of friends and acquaintances picked up along the way. A Bernstein visit was always a festive occasion. When he had been drinking – this occurred with increasing regularity in later years – I became on occasion his long-lost friend and confidant to whom he would open his heart, leaving me feeling a little like Charlie Chaplin in *City Lights*, the tramp who is befriended by a drunken millionaire who does not recognize him when he is sober. During the Edinburgh Festival of 1973, CBS acted as host at a special party to celebrate Bernstein's fifty-fifth birthday. By the end of the evening, shedding real tears on my shoulder, Bernstein complained bitterly that he was only two years younger than Beethoven at the time of his death, and had still not created a lasting musical work by which to be remembered. I recall a number of other such occasions with affection, regretting only that I could not offer greater solace. It was difficult to tell whether his frustration was with himself for failing to write a masterpiece, or with the failure of the public and, even more so, the press, to recognize fully his qualities as a composer.

Leonard Bernstein was an important composer of the twentieth century, despite his own self-doubts and the churlishness of some of the critics of his day. I believe that his music will continue to be heard long after his many friends and protégés have ceased to proselytize on his behalf. It is my hope that this book may persuade readers to rediscover or explore that music more fully.

Paul Myers
London, 1998

I

A young man with a brilliant
future – Bernstein at the
piano rehearses for a
performance at Lewisohn
Stadium, New York, c. 1944.

*One didn't know from which springboard he
would dive, but one knew there would be a hell
of a splash.*

Marc Blitzstein, in the New York *Post*

The Early Years 1918–45

This is not a rags-to-riches story. Louis Bernstein was born on 25 August 1918, to Samuel and Jennie Bernstein in the town of Lawrence, Massachusetts, north of Boston. At that time Sam Bernstein was an ambitious clerk in the firm of Frankel and Smith, wholesalers to barbers and dealers in wigs in the New England area. Louis was the first of three children. He was registered with this name to honour the memory of Jennie's grandfather, but as neither of his parents liked it, he was called Leonard or Lenny from the start. (Years later, Bernstein returned to Lawrence to make the change official in the local register.) Throughout Bernstein's childhood and teenage years, which included the Stock Market crash and the Depression, his father's business prospered and the family changed homes or acquired new houses with some regularity, often moving several times in the same year. The real rags-to-riches saga is in fact Sam Bernstein's, and it is important to recognize it in order to understand the complex and sometimes turbulent relationship between father and son.

Sam, born Shmuel Yosef ben Yehuda, the son of a Hasidic scholar-rabbi, was a penniless Russian who, with the help of an uncle who had settled in America a few years earlier, escaped the *pogroms* or, worse, conscription into the brutally-run Tsarist military service. In 1908 he entered the United States via the United Hebrews Charity in Danzig and, thence, a boat from Liverpool to New York. Like many Jews whose first image of the 'Land of the Free' had been the Statue of Liberty and the lower end of Manhattan Island, Shmuel, sixteen years old, speaking no English and having survived the appalling conditions of travelling steerage, was renamed Samuel Joseph Bernstein by an immigration official on Ellis Island.

Despite his ignorance of the language, the newly dubbed Samuel was a reasonably well-educated young man. As the eldest son, he had been to a religious primary school, moving on to the *yeshiva*, or rabbinical college, to study the Torah and the Talmud. His departure from Russia had been a severe disappointment to his parents – they

The Statue of Liberty as it appeared to immigrants on Ellis Island in the early years of the century

had hoped he would follow in his father's footsteps as a religious scholar, but he had left in secret without warning them.

Once Uncle Harry Levy (né Herschel Malamud), a barber by profession, had paid the necessary twenty-five-dollar bond on his behalf (in case he fell foul of the authorities and had to be repatriated), Samuel had to find a job. The only work available was in the squalor of the Fulton Fish Market in lower Manhattan and he earned a pittance in the humblest of tasks, gutting and trimming fish. But, like so many immigrants of that era, he was tough, resilient and determined. He survived every obstacle and indignity, and with an obstinate mixture of diligence and enterprise, coupled with some bold gambles and a share of good luck, he carved a niche for himself in middle-class Jewish America. Initially, he existed on tips from customers (a few coins in the equivalent of a begging plate), but moved on to steady work which earned him five dollars for a seventy-two-hour working week. He took English classes at night, and tried but failed to pass the Post Office examinations, with the aim of becoming a postman. (He never mastered the English language perfectly, and his occasional malapropisms in later years were a source of good-natured family amusement.)

By good fortune, Harry Levy's barbershop was successful and, after four harsh years in New York, Sam was rescued from the privations and the fetor of the Fulton Market, moving to Hartford, Connecticut, to work for his uncle. It wasn't long before Sam was offered a better job as a stock clerk for Frankel and Smith and, when a new branch was opened in Boston, he moved there. By 1917, Sam Bernstein, already an American citizen, had become Assistant Manager at Frankel and Smith, with a salary of fifteen dollars a week and was ready to find a wife and start a family. After a brief courtship, he married Jennie Resnick, also an immigrant from Russia, who had been employed in the wool factories at Lawrence since the age of twelve.

It was an unhappy arrangement from the start. Sam retained his love of traditional Hebrew studies, and his life was dictated by his religion, his business ambitions and his determination to achieve social acceptance and status. Jennie, who had left school to work at the mill, was not an intellectual. Where Sam was serious to the point of dourness, forever correct and respectable in his clothes and manners, she was pretty, charming, frivolous and intelligently bright but lacking true education. While Sam's head remained buried in the Torah, she read romantic novels and popular magazines, and it is more than likely that she married him because he provided an escape from life at the mill.

They moved into an apartment in a shabby working-class district of Boston and, ten months later, Louis/Leonard was born (back in Lawrence, though, as Jennie had returned there to be with her mother during the final weeks of her pregnancy). Samuel was contemptuous of his in-laws. He brought Jennie and Leonard, who was a sickly infant, back to Boston, and excluded the Resnicks from his home.

Sam and Jennie argued constantly, usually about money and her spendthrift housekeeping, and she left him on several occasions, only to be persuaded to return by her own family. All three children – Leonard, Shirley Anne (born in 1923) and Burton (born in 1932) – were conscious of growing up in a tense, unhappy atmosphere, and the two Bernstein operas that are coupled in *A Quiet Place* reflect the malaise and disappointments of a loveless couple. (The husband and central figure is called Sam. His wife is Dinah, the name of Leonard's paternal grandmother, and the libretto contains, by reference, some episodes that are embarrassingly similar to his own life.)

As time passed, Samuel's business ventures continued to flourish. In 1920 he was promoted to Manager of the Boston office and by 1923 felt confident enough to set up on his own as the Samuel Bernstein Hair Company, supplier of wigs and beauty products throughout the area. In 1927, an astute acquisition – the local franchise of the newly invented Frederics Permanent Wave Machine – helped to make his company the most successful of its kind in New England. With each new move of his 'upwardly mobile' career, the family changed homes and Samuel became a model citizen, a pillar of the local synagogue, and living proof of The American Dream.

As a Hasidic Jew (the Hasidim being the followers of Baal Shem Tov, an eighteenth-century mystic who persuaded his followers that their religion should be a joyful experience), Samuel Bernstein had been raised in a tradition in which singing and dancing were as much a part of religious life as contemplative thought and earnest study. The young Leonard grew up with the melodies of ancient Hasidic tunes, brought to Europe from the Holy Land via Turkey and North Africa, which his father would sing to himself around the house. The Boston *shul* was on the other side of the town and, for practical reasons, Samuel took his family to Temple Mishkan Tefila in the suburb of Roxbury where they were living. It was a conservative (as opposed to orthodox) synagogue, which permitted men and women to sit to-gether, and Sam soon became an active member of the congregation, involving himself in community ventures.

There are conflicting stories of how early Leonard discovered and fell in love with music. Fond family reminiscences suggest that, even as a tiny tot, he would beg to hear music, either on the piano in various friends' houses, or on his mother's wind-up Victrola, with its

The newly invented electric
permanent wave machine

varied assortment of 78 rpm records that ranged from Jewish cantors
to popular songs and operatic excepts. From the age of six he attended
the excellent William Lloyd Garrison School in Roxbury, where the
teachers taught the rudiments of singing and music-reading, and he
enjoyed hours of entertainment via the new medium of radio, with its
pot-pourri of the latest hits, commercial jingles and signature tunes.

   Probably the greatest influence was the music heard each week at
Temple Mishkan Tefila which, in addition to the tenor cantor singing
traditional melodies, boasted an organ and a choir. Many of
Bernstein's works are influenced either by Judaism or Jewish musical

traditions, most notably in the symphonies *Jeremiah* and *Kaddish*, in the ballet *Dybbuk*, in *Chichester Psalms, Hashkiveinu*, Concerto for Orchestra (incorporating *Jubilee Games*) and one or two unexpected places.

Strangely, he was not encouraged to learn to play a musical instrument from a very young age – a normal aspect of a child's education in most middle-class Jewish families – and he began at the relatively late age of ten, when an aunt, moving from the Boston area to live in Brooklyn, gave the Bernsteins a sofa and an upright piano. For Leonard, the piano was a pivotal acquisition, and he later claimed that, from that moment, he knew that music would be his life.

A local girl, Frieda Karp, was hired for one dollar an hour to give him lessons. He made unusually rapid progress, quickly absorbing simple training exercises and moving on to Chopin, some of the easier Bach and other classics. His appetite for all music was voracious and he devoted additional hours to experimenting and discovering the rudiments of harmony for himself by learning how to reproduce the popular music he heard on the radio.

Within three years, Frieda admitted that she could take Leonard no further with his studies and recommended that he find a teacher at the New England Conservatory of Music in Boston. In 1930, Leonard selected Susan Williams. Her fee was three dollars an hour and this triggered the first of many battles that were to occur over the next decade between father and son.

Sam Bernstein had struggled all his life to make something of himself and he was determined that his son should have all the opportunities that he had never enjoyed. Academically, Leonard was always a high achiever. In 1929 he had graduated from the William Lloyd Garrison School to the famous Boston Latin School, founded in 1635 and one of the oldest and finest in the country, whose pupils had included many distinguished statesmen from Benjamin Franklin to John F. Kennedy, and writers such as Ralph Waldo Emerson and George Santayana. If Leonard continued with the same application and success, he would also be guaranteed a place at Harvard University. Sam hoped, understandably, that his elder son would one day take over his thriving Hair Company. He had never invested in the Stock Market, and so had survived the Crash of 1929 that had wiped out so many business enterprises. Despite the privations of the

Depression, middle-class American women still wanted permanent waves and beauty treatment and his company continued to prosper. Alternatively, as the grandson of a rabbi and the son of a devout student of the Talmud, Leonard could devote himself to religious studies or academic pursuits, occupations that Sam was in a position to support financially.

Music, on the other hand, while being a pleasant and artistic pastime (though constant and enthusiastic hammering on Aunt Clara's old upright piano disturbed the peace of the household), was out of the question as a serious occupation. Sam Bernstein could certainly afford to pay the necessary three dollars an hour for piano lessons, but he sensed with some concern that his son considered himself a putative professional musician. In the world of the Russian ghetto from which he had come (and even in his occasional encounters with them in the United States), musicians were *klezmers*: layabouts and drifters, who played at weddings or Bar Mitzvahs for a handful of coins. They were neither intellectuals nor serious men of commerce, and it was inconceivable that all Sam's years of struggle should be rewarded by a son who, in his eyes, would be little more than a street beggar.

In *A Quiet Place*, one of the subjects explored is the failure of the father and his son to express the deep love they feel for one another. At the time of the three-dollar piano lesson crisis, Samuel Bernstein was trying to protect his son from a future that he himself did not comprehend. Leonard, filled with self-pity and misconstruing his father's intentions, felt only resentment and childish hatred. Years later, he publicly acknowledged his mistake. His father, proud of his world-famous son's achievements, summed up his feelings with the often-quoted 'How did I know he was going to become Leonard Bernstein?'

In the end, Leonard prevailed, subsidizing his father's reduced weekly allowance (cut back to accommodate the increased cost of lessons) by giving piano lessons to local children, and by forming a small jazz group with some of his friends to earn a few extra dollars at local weekend 'gigs'. Ironically, Susan Williams proved to be a disastrous choice as a piano teacher. She pronounced Leonard's keyboard technique to be woefully inadequate and introduced him to a misguided system that she had developed herself, which could have ruined his playing and which took some years to correct! His studies with her are probably best forgotten, except for one significant development: a piano concerto, never completed, but ambitiously called *The War of the Gypsies and the Russians*. He had embarked on his career as a composer.

Throughout his early years, Leonard made friends with people to whom he would remain loyal for the rest of his life. Perhaps the earliest of these was Sid Ramin, a few months younger than himself, whom he met at the age of twelve and with whom he shared many of his innermost secrets and ambitions. He gave Ramin his first piano lessons and, years later, Ramin was one of the orchestrators of *West Side Story*. Later still, having enjoyed a distinguished career in the popular music field, Ramin would advise the composer on the rock instrumentation for *Mass*, and was again called upon for the final orchestration of *A Quiet Place*. However, back in 1932, they were playing four-hand arrangements of popular tunes and jazz classics like *St Louis Blues*, and learned Gershwin's *Rhapsody in Blue* together.

Needless to say, Sid was always kept fully informed of Leonard's anguish with his father, whom he claimed to hate for his opposition to his musical studies. But it is more than likely that the real cause of his antipathy towards Sam was the continuing conflict between his parents. For the most part rejected by her husband, Jennie lavished her affections on their eldest son, and both Leonard and his sister Shirley spoke in later years of times when they had come to their mother's aid because family squabbles had reached breaking-point. On one occasion, when Leonard was twelve, a breakfast-table request for a small amount of money for Shirley caused Sam to explode with anger and pick up a glass milk-bottle, as if to hit Jennie with it. She fled to another room and Leonard stood at the door, his arms spread, refusing to let his father pass.

There was also a strong element of childish dramatic exaggeration. For his Bar Mitzvah in 1931 (at which Leonard delivered his speech in both English and Hebrew), his father generously gave him a Chickering baby grand piano and a cruise on the Panama Canal. In fact, after the initial drama subsided, there was an uneasy period of 'armed neutrality' between them, tempered by efforts on both sides at reconciliation. While Sam disapproved of his son's musical aspirations, he was immensely proud of his achievements, and he vacillated between supporting Leonard's efforts and damning them. He began taking Leonard to orchestral concerts in Boston, which was a new experience for both of them. Later, his beauty company sponsored a series of fifteen-minute piano recitals by the seventeen-year-old Leonard on a local Boston radio station. And yet, he wrote to his son's new teacher, Helen Coates, to explain that a professional musical career was out of the question.

The arrival of Helen Coates in Leonard's life was an important event, marking another association that would last for more than half a century. Originally, Leonard had approached Heinrich Gebhard, the most distinguished piano teacher in Boston, who had studied with the great Theodor Leschetizky. Gebhard, however, recommended his assistant, Helen, a young woman in her twenties, who, to Sam's relief, charged a much lower fee. (He was resigned to paying for further and more expensive lessons.) In addition to repairing the damage done by Susan Williams's 'keyboard method', Helen taught, guided and encouraged her pupil. She became his confidante and the recipient of myriad letters and postcards over the years, describing his latest triumphs. Throughout his life, Bernstein was a prolific correspondent, always finding time in his endlessly busy schedule to maintain regular contact with a number of friends. Eventually 'Miss Coates', as she was always known, became his personal secretary and a Scylla past which no Bernstein visitor could travel without approval. Over the next few years, Leonard consolidated his musical education. He discovered and devoured new pieces avidly, seemingly dividing his time between the piano and his local music shop. At the same time, he maintained high academic standards at Boston Latin, where his education was far broader than that of a highly talented music student working his way through the lower levels of a conservatory.

Sam Bernstein's business continued to expand and, in 1932, he built a summer house for the family in Sharon, Massachusetts. During holidays there, Leonard organized a group of friends known as The Sharon Players to put on shows of Gilbert and Sullivan and even a pastiche of Bizet's *Carmen* (long before Oscar Hammerstein's *Carmen Jones*) that was filled with parochial references to amuse local friends and families. His passion for music encompassed every style.

His father had introduced him to orchestral concerts via the Boston Pops and Arthur Fiedler, but in 1933 Leonard and a friend bought subscriptions to the Boston Symphony's season, where he discovered and fell under the spell of the orchestra's conductor, Serge Koussevitzky. A flamboyant and colourful character, Koussevitzky's readings of the classical masterpieces were remarkable for their emotional intensity and dramatic style. Coming to Boston from Russia in 1924 and remaining there until his death in 1951, Koussevitzky became a major influence on American musical life, sponsoring some of the most important works of the twentieth century. There is no question that Bernstein modelled himself on the great Russian conductor, both in the intensity of his own performances and the sense of 'gala' or 'occasion' he would bring to every concert.

Having graduated with high marks, he was accepted by Harvard in 1935 as a music major. The choice of Harvard appears to have been something of a compromise, possibly to assuage his father for, while it offered the highest intellectual stimuli a student could ask for (as well as invaluable business 'contacts' among the children of the rich and powerful), Harvard's musical standards fell far below those of the more established music conservatories such as New York's Juilliard School or the Curtis Institute in Philadelphia. He still had to decide on the form his musical career would follow (it is interesting to note in passing that his first completed composition was the valedictory *Class Song*, composed for Boston Latin). At Harvard, he took a general music course under Professor Arthur Tillman Merritt, later adding advanced harmony and fugue with the composer Walter Piston, together with courses in English Literature, Fine Arts and German. His piano studies continued privately, 'graduating' to Heinrich Gebhard, who helped greatly to expand his musical understanding and appreciation.

During his Harvard years, like many brilliant students, he did not appear to study very assiduously, but participated enthusiastically in many university activities. He joined the famous Glee Club, and played squash regularly. It was a sport he enjoyed and played for the rest of his active life. He also took up the energetic pastime of rowing a one-man skiff. Although he lived on campus, he still went home regularly to attend synagogue, to maintain contact with old friends and to spend time with his family. As a baby and during early childhood, he had never enjoyed good health, but he outgrew these

childish weaknesses. But his suffering from asthma did not inhibit his passion for smoking, which he took up as a teenager and which dogged him for the rest of his life.

Throughout Leonard Bernstein's career, certain years could be described as crucial in that the events that occurred would have a lifelong effect. The first of these was 1937, when he was still a teenager; in this year he would encounter three people who would have a major influence upon him. In January he met Dimitri Mitropoulos, the conductor whose flamboyant podium style strongly influenced Bernstein's own. Mitropoulos was the guest of honour at an exclusive Harvard tea-party, and there are various stories about Bernstein's presence on that occasion. According to Humphrey Burton, Bernstein was an invited guest, but Meryle Secrest, in her biography of the composer, maintains that Bernstein told a friend (Robert Lubell) that he was going to gatecrash the event. Perhaps the most charming version came from Bernstein himself many years later in a *New Yorker* article, in which he claimed that his car had run out of petrol outside the Harvard Hellenistic Society's building. He had not planned to attend the tea-party, but as he was there, decided that he might as well go in. His meeting with Mitropoulos was therefore dictated by fate!

The forty-year-old Mitropoulos, who made no secret of his homosexuality, had a hypnotic effect on the impressionable younger man, who was clearly uncertain at that time of his own sexual inclinations. There is, however, nothing to confirm that a physical relationship ever took place between them. It is more likely that the conductor, aware of the effect he was having on the star-struck Bernstein, indulged in mild flirtation. Less friendly biographers maintain that one seduced the other, or vice versa. Bernstein later dramatized his meeting with the older man in a clearly autobiographical short story, in which little more than the names were changed, underlining his admiration and also suggesting a homosexual attraction between them. At the time of their first meetings, when Mitropoulos invited Leonard to attend his rehearsals (and revealed a whole new musical world to him), he encouraged him to fulfil his stated ambition to be a composer. Later, he sponsored his conducting lessons under Fritz Reiner at the Curtis Institute in Philadelphia.

That summer, Leonard forsook the family home at Sharon to take a job as a music counsellor at Camp Onota in Massachusetts. Summer

Opposite, an early picture of Bernstein conducting; for many years, emulating his idol Dimitri Mitropoulos, Bernstein conducted without a baton.

camp, a tradition for most American teenage town-dwellers during the long, hot months, offered modestly paid employment for hundreds of late-teen/early-twenties students, and Leonard was there to organize and supervise various musical activities. This included a production of *The Pirates of Penzance*, in which the role of the Pirate King was assigned to Adolph Green, two years Bernstein's junior. They became immediate and permanent friends. Green and his writing partner, Betty Comden (one of Broadway's and Hollywood's most successful partnerships), would provide the lyrics for *On the Town* and *Wonderful Town*, and continued to work with Bernstein on various other projects for the rest of his life.

In the autumn of the same year, Bernstein made his first professional appearance as a concert pianist, performing Ravel's Piano Concerto with the State Symphony Orchestra in Cambridge, Massachusetts. He received encouraging reviews, which may have persuaded him that, despite his limited repertoire, he had the talent to become a full-time pianist. At his age, many would-be professional pianists could already boast half a dozen concertos and several solid recital programmes, but he had only the Ravel concerto and a limited number of well-known solo items. His career plans were still undecided, other than that he was determined to be a success, come what may.

It would be wrong to suggest that Bernstein at this point was a dilettante musician. His brilliance, coupled with an ability to absorb everything quickly, allowed him to move rapidly from one musical project to the next without feeling the need to consolidate his keyboard repertoire. One of his personal 'warhorse' showpieces, although not popular with his student colleagues, was a craggy set of Piano Variations by Aaron Copland, one of America's most important composers. By pure accident – and if one is to believe Bernstein's critics, very few of his important 'connections' were accidental – he found himself sitting next to Copland in a New York theatre on 14 November 1937. They were introduced and Bernstein was invited back to Copland's apartment for the latter's thirty-seventh birthday party.

It was the beginning of a long and important friendship. Copland, who was a central figure in New York intellectual circles, introduced the starry-eyed Leonard to many famous musicians, writers and poets. Although Mitropoulos gave financial support, it was also Copland who persuaded Bernstein that he should become a conductor. And he offered invaluable and constructive advice when Bernstein started to work as a serious composer. Himself a protégé of Koussevitzky (who was anxious to sponsor an American school of composers), Copland later effected Leonard's introduction to the great Boston maestro. For many years, they maintained an active and warm correspondence, during much of which Copland was the mentor and Bernstein the enthusiastic acolyte.

After the heady encounters of 1937, Bernstein concentrated on his Harvard studies for a while. He displayed yet another talent as music editor of the *Harvard Advocate* in 1938, writing reviews and commentaries that were both incisive and provocative. He had not heard again from Dimitri Mitropoulos, but a letter sent to Minneapolis, where the conductor was in residence, was immediately followed by an invitation to visit and they spent a week together, during which Bernstein sight-read scores, attended rehearsals and learned a little more of the spiritual values that the older man believed he should invest in his music. It was also flattering for the young Bernstein, not yet twenty, to find himself dubbed by Mitropoulos a 'genius boy'.

He continued to work at the piano, giving his first full-length recital in the summer of that year, at which he played his own *Music for the Dance No. 1*, inspired by the dancer Anna Sokolow. But he did not complete any composition, despite encouragement from Aaron Copland. When he returned to Harvard in the autumn, however, he was invited to write music for the Greek Society's new production of *The Birds* by Aristophanes, which would be presented at the end of the school year. Another significant event of that year was the arrival of Copland himself in October, to help supervise the American première of his *El salón México* by the Boston Symphony under Koussevitzky. Bernstein was enthralled with the music and begged Copland for the opportunity to study with him. For the moment anyway, he was convinced that he too should become a composer, and believed that his friend's support was conclusive proof that he had the talent. Copland's reply was, as ever, guardedly enthusiastic.

The Birds was presented in April of 1939. The score consisted of about forty minutes of incidental music, including occasional fanfares, for chamber orchestra, harp and percussion, and the two performances were played to full if somewhat academic houses (it was performed in Greek). Also present were Helen Coates and Aaron Copland, who witnessed Leonard Bernstein's successful début as a conductor.

In 1938 Bernstein had seen a controversial Brechtian music-drama on Broadway called *The Cradle Will Rock*. It was by Marc Blitzstein, who once described himself: 'Number one, I'm a Jew. Number two, I'm a Communist. Number three, I'm a homo composer.' *The Cradle Will Rock* had been directed by Orson Welles and produced by John Houseman (whose later collaboration would produce the classic film *Citizen Kane*) but, because of its left-wing sympathies, the show had almost been closed by the authorities on the first night, and was saved only when the entire cast, accompanied by about a thousand members

Marc Blitzstein (1905–64), whose approach to American music-theatre strongly influenced the young Bernstein

of the audience, marched across New York to perform it in another theatre. It had been an overnight success. Bernstein persuaded his colleagues in the Harvard Dramatic Club to put on their own production of *Cradle*, and found enthusiastic support for the venture in the faculty of the university. The whole production was mounted in something like ten days and, forever confident, Bernstein invited Marc Blitzstein to attend the first night. Blitzstein arrived for the dress rehearsal and, within a short time, recognized a kindred spirit in Bernstein. He was reminded of himself at the same age and was charmed by the younger man's boundless talent and enthusiasm. He stayed behind for the cast party after the show, taking turns at the piano with Bernstein.

The Harvard production was handsomely praised by the *Boston Globe* and Bernstein himself enjoyed the lion's share of the plaudits. More important, however, was the influence that Blitzstein seemed to exert over the young Bernstein, who was entranced with both the man and his music which, coupled with that of Copland, seemed to epitomize the original *American* musical voice that he sought. Blitzstein had developed an American form of the socially conscious music-theatre established by Eisler, Brecht and Weill in Europe (this appealed to Bernstein's high-minded liberal conscience), and he might perhaps have enjoyed greater notoriety and respect if the United States had not moved increasingly to the right and into the artistic abyss of the McCarthy era. Today the bulk of Marc Blitzstein's music is hardly known. There are a few recordings of some of his major stage works and his *Airborne Symphony* was performed and recorded by Bernstein with the New York Philharmonic in later years. He died tragically in 1964, murdered on the island of Martinique in what, according to *Grove's Dictionary of Music and Musicians'* diplomatic description, '... appeared to be a political argument'. Reports at the time suggested that he was beaten to death by homophobic servicemen whom he had mistakenly propositioned.

Bernstein graduated *cum laude* rather than *magna cum laude* from Harvard, probably because he had sailed casually through his classes, finding academic chores less than demanding. His father offered him one hundred dollars a week, no mean sum in 1939, to join the family business, but he set that aside and chose instead to move to New York. Once there, he shared an apartment in Greenwich Village with his friend Adolph Green from Camp Onota days. Green had formed a group, including the actress Judy Holliday and his co-writer Betty Comden, called The Revuers, who performed satirical songs and sketches at The Village Vanguard. Bernstein's own career was still not taking any particular direction and he divided his time between bohemian Greenwich Village and Aaron Copland's more elegant circle of friends farther uptown. He made a piano transcription of Copland's *El salón México*, and began work on a *Hebrew Song* for mezzo-soprano and orchestra, using a text from The Lamentations of Jeremiah, which would eventually become his first Symphony, subtitled *Jeremiah*.

At the end of the summer, Bernstein returned to Boston, having found no permanent employment. Encouraged by Copland, Roy Harris (an American composer sponsored by Koussevitzky) and William Schuman (one of Copland's composition students), he considered further studies as a conductor, but an application to the

The distinguished conductor Fritz Reiner, under whom Bernstein studied at the Curtis Institute in Philadelphia. He also engaged the young composer to conduct the première of his First Symphony in Pittsburgh in 1944.

Juilliard School in New York had been unsucccessful. Copland came to the rescue by arranging a meeting with Fritz Reiner of the Curtis Institute in Philadelphia (by far the best choice in the country), and Reiner promised to give him an examination in late September. At about the same time, Mitropoulos reappeared in his life, offering the same encouragement and helping to point him towards the podium. Bernstein was accepted by the Curtis Institute, with a scholarship to cover his tuition, and when his father refused to continue paying for his maintenance, Mitropoulos provided a monthly living allowance.

The Curtis Institute was ideal for Bernstein, since it encouraged both composers and performers. The composers Samuel Barber and Gian-Carlo Menotti had both studied there, as had the pianists Shura Cherkassky and Jorge Bolet. Bernstein studied orchestration with the composer Randall Thompson, score-reading with Renée Longy Miquelle and conducting with Reiner. His piano studies (in a department headed by Rudolf Serkin) were with Isabelle Vengerova. Several of his fellow students were to become lifelong colleagues and friends, including the composer-conductor Lukas Foss and the composer-orchestrator Hershy Kay, who would later help to score *On the Town*, *Candide* and *Mass*.

In the summer of the following year – 1940 – Bernstein was to work with his third great conducting model, Serge Koussevitzky. The Berkshire Music Center at Tanglewood, one of America's great summer teaching institutions, was having its first season, with Copland sharing composition classes with Paul Hindemith, and Koussevitzky in charge of conducting. With recommendations from all his friends, Bernstein was immediately accepted.

The summer was an unqualified success for Bernstein, who quickly revealed his musical talents – from score-reading to conducting – and used his considerable charm to endear himself to Koussevitzky. He was soon adopted by the conductor and would have remained with him in Boston had not Reiner intervened angrily, pointing out that the Curtis scholarship still had a further year to run. In that era, rivalry between musicians was far more noticeable than it is today (the age-old feud between the violinists Mischa Elman and Jascha Heifetz spawned dozens of good anecdotes, many of them apocryphal), and even distinguished conductors were not above a little in-fighting when it came to protecting their interests in a clearly brilliant protégé like

Following page, Bernstein (third from left) studied orchestration at Curtis with the composer Randall Thompson. Also in the class were (from left) Waldemar Dabrowski, Leo Luskin, Hershy Kay, Albert Falkove and Constant Vauclain. Seated are Dr Thompson and Annette Elkanova.

Bernstein. It was therefore no surprise that the ill-tempered Reiner would castigate Koussevitzky for trying to lure away his 'star' pupil. (There had also been a disappointing incident with Mitropoulos, who had offered Bernstein a job as an assistant in Minneapolis, but had been forced to withdraw it due to resistance by his orchestra.) Before returning to Philadelphia for the new term, Bernstein again turned his attention to composing, with a Sonata for Violin and Piano. Influenced by jazz and Aaron Copland's musical style, it was little more than a student effort, and Bernstein's feelings for the piece cooled over the years. It was never published, but he later incorporated some of its themes in his ballet *Facsimile* and his *Age of Anxiety* Symphony. Early in 1941, however, he received twenty-five dollars from Boosey & Hawkes for his piano transcription of Copland's *El salón México*. It was the first published musical work to bear his name.

It is difficult to assess when Bernstein's first homosexual encounter took place. With a strong sexual drive throughout his life, he may have experimented with teenagers like himself, and it must be remembered that in the 1930s such activity was still regarded as a perversion, carrying with it a sense of guilt and shame. During his teenage years and well into his twenties, Bernstein remained sexually ambivalent. He was nineteen when he met the overtly homosexual Mitropoulos, who was an idol and possible role-model, and if he did not enter a liaison with the conductor in the spring of 1937, he almost certainly did later in the same year with Aaron Copland, who became, somewhat against his will, his literary 'father confessor'.

Nevertheless, Bernstein remained sexually and emotionally uncommitted. In the autumn of 1940, while at Curtis, he formed a deep friendship with a sixteen-year-old schoolgirl, Shirley Gabis, to whom he opened his heart. Nothing came of their relationship, although she conceded that there was 'heat' between them. He told her that he had a 'canker' in his soul and, almost at the same time, wrote to Copland about his most recent sexual adventures with a young (male) painter. Bernstein also admitted in later years to a brief affair with his score-reading teacher Renée Longy Miquelle, although whatever seduction took place appears to have been initiated by her. In the summer of 1941, while at Tanglewood, he was seriously involved with an attractive young woman called Kiki Speyer and, encouraged by Koussevitzky, even discussed marriage. By the end of the festival, however, he fled alone to Key West, writing to Copland that he was going to 'get away' from people and Kiki. 'I confessed all,' he wrote, 'and she wants to marry me anyway ...' For the most part, there were very few women in Bernstein's life, but countless men.

Bernstein's final year at Curtis was busier than ever, including a trip to Chicago to attend rehearsals of Reiner's performance of *Der Rosenkavalier*, and with concentrated studies on every front. He graduated with A+ and A in every subject (reputedly the only A ever given by Reiner). Between graduating and his second summer at Tanglewood, he returned to Harvard to compose a score for the Student Union production of *The Peace* by Aristophanes, conducting the performances in May. He also won a music quiz organized by a Boston paper, which gave a cash prize of $150, together with the opportunity to conduct the Boston Pops Orchestra in an open-air concert. It was Bernstein's début with a professional orchestra and he acquitted himself well with a performance of the overture to Wagner's *Die Meistersinger*. The conductor Harry Ellis Dickson was present and described Bernstein as a 'natural'. The concert took place on Friday 11 June 1941, at the Esplanade – a large, open-air venue on the banks of

Serge Koussevitsky – Bernstein's conducting 'godfather' and a major influence on his musical life

the Charles River. Perhaps auguring his future career, he appeared before an audience of about 22,000 people.

At that time, America anticipated being drawn into the European war and, while at Tanglewood, Bernstein received the draft board questionnaire that was sent to all young men of military age. He was, however, deferred because of his continuing asthma.

With his studies complete, Bernstein found himself facing the realities of looking for employment. Although Koussevitzky, who had become a father-figure in Bernstein's life, wanted him to remain in Boston as an untitled assistant, Bernstein was trapped in a catch-22 situation. The Boston Symphony Orchestra was the last non-union orchestra in America, but if Bernstein worked there, he would be banned from working elsewhere with unionized orchestras.

It was a difficult period in Bernstein's life. He had talent to burn, but nobody was making use of it. Like many creative artists, he had endured bouts of depression, which could easily be displaced by soaring elation when a job came along. He took various teaching and accompanying assignments and rejoined his friends Comden, Green and Judy Holliday who were in a musical, *My Dear Public*, written by Irving Caesar and Gerald Marx. The show was a failure, but the veteran Caesar, who had worked with the young Gershwin, recognized Bernstein's talent, and promised to help find him a job in New York.

Bernstein continued a desultory musical existence through the first half of 1942, with time to work on *Jeremiah* and to complete a clarinet sonata, started a year earlier. The first performance of the sonata was in Boston that April. Its style has been compared with that of Hindemith, who had been at Tanglewood, although most of the music, especially the faster, slightly jazzy movement, is more reminiscent of Bernstein's guide and mentor, Aaron Copland.

For his third summer at Tanglewood, Bernstein served as Koussevitzky's assistant in conducting classes, and in the autumn of that year decided to try his luck again in New York. He worked with The Revuers in Greenwich Village and as a rehearsal pianist for dancers. In addition, Irving Caesar made good his promise of regular work by introducing him to the publishers Harms-Witmark, owned by Warner Brothers, who hired him on a weekly salary to make piano arrangements of 'novelty' orchestra pieces, as well as noting down the improvisations on records by various well-known jazz musicians.

Bernstein (and some of his biographers) considered this work 'demeaning', although by doing it he learned a great deal about the everyday mechanics of the popular music world. His efforts were published under the pseudonym Lenny Amber ('amber' being the English translation of the German *bernstein*). Obviously, he was destined for greater things, but it might also be remembered that Arnold Schoenberg – an equally unlikely candidate for such work – had earned a living by orchestrating operettas (the popular music of his time) in Berlin at the turn of the century. In fact, Harms proved to be a very beneficial association. Frank Campbell Watson, the chief editor, showed real interest in Bernstein's own music, and arranged a five-year contract, with advances against future royalties, that doubled his weekly income and guaranteed immediate publication of his Clarinet Sonata.

With his income fortified, Bernstein was able to live in a bigger and better apartment by sharing it with an artist called Edys Merrill, a friend of Adolph Green's ex-wife, whose war effort involved working in a factory. Aaron Copland, forever present to offer help, paid for a rented Steinway grand so that Bernstein could continue to coach singers, rehearse dancers and help The Revuers. Merrill, whose release from the relentless din of the factory floor was replaced by endless piano-playing, singing and dancing in the flat, covered her ears, screaming 'I hate music!' This did not persuade Bernstein to stop, but inspired his song-cycle *I Hate Music*, subtitled *Five Kid Songs for Soprano and Piano*, which he completed in 1942 and dedicated to Merrill. In the autumn of that year, he also completed his first symphony, *Jeremiah*, dedicated to his father, Samuel Bernstein.

The work is in three movements, played without pause, its music based on the Ashkenazic cantillation or intoning of the Bible, which was the traditional method of chanting the liturgy. The first movement, *Prophesy*, expresses a deep, heartfelt solemnity, to be followed by *Profanation* (the corrupt priesthood mocking Jeremiah), a scherzo-like movement with a strong, rhythmic pulse, clearly influenced by jazz. The finale, *Lamentation*, on which he had originally worked as a separate piece, indicates (and musically reflects) that the prophesy of the first movement has been fulfilled; it laments the fall of the city of Jerusalem. Scored for mezzo-soprano and orchestra, the movement is sung in Hebrew and taken from the Book of Lamentations, Chapter i. 1–4, Chapter iv. 14–15, and Chapter v. 20–21.

Bernstein entered the symphony in a competition sponsored by the New England Conservatory of Music, of which Koussevitzky was the main judge. He made the deadline of 31 December in the nick of time, thanks to an army of friends who helped transfer the final orchestration to paper. All works were submitted anonymously. To Bernstein's disappointment, his symphony did not win, but Koussevitzky later consoled him, pointing out that it was, after all, a first effort. (It might also be mentioned at this point that, although he was an excellent conductor and a fine musician, Koussevitzky had never been an adept score-reader, which may have affected his initial judgement of the piece.) In recent years, *Jeremiah* has been performed with some success, and would appear to have survived rather better than the winning piece by Gardner Read, a student of Copland at Tanglewood and of Howard Hanson at the Eastman School.

At the start of 1943, Bernstein's career was not developing very noticeably, but he drew some attention to himself – from the press as well as the audience – in February, when he stepped in at late notice to play the première of Aaron Copland's Piano Sonata at Town Hall (Copland being bound to a contract in Hollywood). This was followed by a discussion, at which Bernstein displayed a ready wit. His father, who happened to be in New York, was also present, and was heard to grumble that, despite the applause and appreciation, his son had earned little money from the exercise.

One of the composers whom Bernstein had met in Copland's circle was Paul Bowles, and in the spring of 1943, he finally made his New York conducting début with a performance of Bowles's opera *The Wind Remains*, to a text by Lorca, at the Museum of Modern Art. It was a major event, with choreography by the young Merce Cunningham and sets by Oliver Smith (who would later work on many Bernstein productions). Virgil Thomson – another admirer from the Copland circle – singled out Bernstein's conducting in his review.

The name Leonard Bernstein was becoming known to New York's classical 'insiders', to the extent that Artur Rodzinski, the new Music Director of the New York Philharmonic, who had previously directed the Cleveland Orchestra, was already considering inviting him to be his assistant when his autumn season opened. Bernstein knew nothing of this, but was kept occupied with a few minor conducting engagements in New York and Boston. More exciting still for him was the news that Harms would publish his *Jeremiah* Symphony and Fritz Reiner would programme its première in Pittsburgh later in the year, either conducting it himself or inviting Bernstein as a guest conductor. In the summer, having heard the symphony again, Koussevitzky now expressed delighted approval, and promised a performance in Boston, following Reiner's première.

Two further important events occurred. When assisting Koussevitzky in a lecture series in Lenox, Massachusetts (Tanglewood was cancelled that summer because of the war), Bernstein met the mezzo-soprano Jennie Tourel, to whom he would be devoted for the rest of her life. He had brought his charming but jazzy *I Hate Music* songs with him, but Koussevitzky strongly disapproved of them. Being a maestro of the old school, he could never accept that jazz should be incorporated into 'serious' classical music (and was angry in later years when his protégé enjoyed success on Broadway). He forbade Tourel and Bernstein to include the songs in her recital. Tourel did as she was told, but then sang them as encore pieces!

The following day Bernstein was summoned to nearby Stockbridge, where Artur Rodzinski offered him the post of assistant conductor at the New York Philharmonic. Always an eccentric man (who was reputed to carry a revolver in his trouser pocket whenever he conducted), Rodzinski explained that he had consulted God as to which conductor to invite, and God had told him, 'Take Bernstein!' Whatever the Almighty's advice, there was a war on at the time, and many possible candidates were serving in the armed forces, so it had been Bernstein's good fortune that his poor health made him medically unfit and therefore available. In addition, the New York Philharmonic's affairs were controlled by Arthur Judson, who also headed the all-powerful Columbia Artists Management and maintained a Svengali-like hold over most of America's major orchestras and their conductors. It is more likely that, under the circumstances, God would have instructed Rodzinski to 'ask Judson'!

In spite of the title, the function of the assistant conductor was relatively modest. As Rodzinski's assistant, Bernstein would be there to go through the many scores submitted to the conductor, to run whatever musical errands were required, to provide occasional help with a rehearsal, including reading through new scores with the orchestra, and similar duties. He was not like the understudy to a leading actor, waiting in the wings to act as a replacement in case of his chief's indisposition. Normally, if the scheduled conductor were not available, his place would be taken by a colleague of similar standing. Nevertheless, the appointment was invaluable to the up-and-coming Bernstein, placing his name on the programmes of the Philharmonic and putting him in direct contact with the powers that controlled musical life in New York.

For an American-trained musician (and a Jew) it was an unexpected honour. Bernstein was interviewed and accepted by Judson, who arranged a reasonable salary and placed him in the hands of his assistant, Bruno Zirato, who had first come to New York as Caruso's secretary and had later been Toscanini's assistant during his time with the New York Philharmonic. Bernstein and his new manager became firm friends, and Zirato also arranged for the young conductor to rent a small apartment in Carnegie Hall itself.

Early into the season Rodzinski was aware that he had chosen a talented assistant and that he was dealing with a very ambitious one. Bernstein had always displayed a certain amount of *chutzpah*. This was the young man who had gatecrashed a party to meet Mitropoulos, who had treated his professors at Harvard in an offhand manner, who had even addressed the formidable Reiner as 'Fritz' (and who in later years would show distinguished composers, including Copland, how to improve their works). Within weeks of his arrival at the Philharmonic, Bernstein was making his presence unnecessarily obvious, to the point that Rodzinski, sensitive to the fact that it was also his own first season in New York, advised Zirato that his protégé was to be banned from circulating and promoting himself in the Green Room after a concert.

But neither Rodzinski nor any other circumstances were going to stand in the way of Bernstein's seemingly inevitable rise. On Saturday 13 November 1943, Jennie Tourel made her New York début at Town Hall and, accompanied by the composer, again sang *I Hate Music*. Bernstein shared in the glowing reviews.

On that same weekend, Artur Rodzinski was taking a mid-season break, and his guest conductor, Bruno Walter, was scheduled to

Bruno Walter (1876–1962), whose indisposition gave Bernstein his opportunity to conduct the New York Philharmonic and enjoy overnight stardom

conduct the New York Philharmonic on the Sunday afternoon in a concert that would be broadcast nationwide. Walter, however, had been taken ill as early as the Friday before, and Bernstein, on Rodzinski's instructions, was told to stand by as his replacement.

Whether it was a generous gesture by Rodzinski (whose own début had occurred as the result of Stokowski's indisposition) or whether Zirato and Judson manipulated the situation by failing to come up with a more suitable replacement will probably never be revealed. Breaking with all previous tradition, and stepping in at the last moment, the 25-year-old Bernstein conducted the broadcast concert with enormous flair. The press – critics and news reporters – had been alerted, and were presented with the sort of heroic stuff of which legends are made. Bernstein made front page news in the *New York Times* and *Herald-Tribune*, and the reviews of the concert were generally excellent. Until that moment, he had been a bright young hopeful, already known in the parochial music circles of Boston and

Bernstein with members of the New York Philharmonic, following his surprise début in November 1943. This photograph appeared in the *New York Times* the day after the concert.

New York. By the following day, he had become a national hero. The New York Philharmonic immediately announced that he would be given the opportunity to conduct the orchestra again and, within a few days, Arthur Judson had received numerous invitations from other American orchestras, eager to hear his brilliant new 'discovery'. Within a week, Bernstein had been interviewed by at least fifteen magazines and newspapers and, in less than a month, the New York Philharmonic was able to use him again, in place of another ailing conductor. Reviews confirmed that he was not a nine-day wonder, and that he was a major new talent.

Bernstein would return to the New York Philharmonic a number of times during that season. More important, however, was the opportunity given by Fritz Reiner for him to conduct the première of his *Jeremiah* Symphony in Pittsburgh early in January of 1944, followed – as Koussevitzky had promised – by his Boston début, again conducting his symphony. He also performed it several times with the New York Philharmonic and, in the spring of that year, the New York Music Critics Circle selected *Jeremiah* as the best new work of the season.

Throughout this period, despite his initial support, Artur Rodzinski became increasingly disenchanted with his assistant, who was clearly carving out a career of his own with little concern for his responsibilities at the New York Philharmonic. The week that Bernstein was making his début in Pittsburgh, Rodzinski fell ill, but his assistant did not return to the city. On another occasion, he absented himself from a Rodzinski rehearsal on the grounds of not feeling well, only to be seen at the barber's and walking his dog. Arthur Judson kept the two men apart by sending Bernstein on a number of guest engagements, and the New York Philharmonic announced that Bernstein would not continue as Rodzinski's assistant, but would be returning to the orchestra the following season as a guest conductor.

The year 1944 was to be an *annus mirabilis* for Bernstein. In the preceding autumn, the young choreographer Jerome Robbins, who was working with the Ballet Theatre, had approached him with the synopsis for a one-act ballet, entitled *Fancy Free*. Robbins explained that he wanted the ballet to be a contemporary New York story involving three sailors on leave for twenty-four hours and their attempts to find themselves some girlfriends. It was the start of a vitally creative partnership between Bernstein and Robbins, later leading to *On the Town*, *West Side Story* and *Dybbuk*.

Using jazz and popular dance rhythms as the basis of the score, Bernstein composed the music between conducting engagements. The Ballet Theatre was on tour during the early part of the year, but Bernstein kept Robbins supplied with each new section by making four-hand piano recordings with Aaron Copland, on which Robbins would phone back or cable his comments. On the company's return to New York, Bernstein attended the rehearsals (often accompanied by his friends Comden and Green), making on-the-spot alterations and improvements to his music according to Robbins's needs.

Oliver Smith was hired to design the moody New York set, and the veteran impressario Sol Hurok presented the ballet at the (old) Metropolitan opera house on Broadway. *Fancy Free* opened on 18 April, with Bernstein conducting, and was an instant success. The audience was captivated by Robbins's vivid and athletic choreography. They were dazzled by its panache and delighted with its moments of genuine humour. Bernstein's score, a mixture of symphonic jazz, Latin rhythms and the immediately accessible melodic appeal of Aaron Copland (whose influence is apparent throughout), was ideally suited

The one-act ballet *Fancy Free*, choreographed by Jerome Robbins. The three sailors were danced by John Kriza, Jerome Robbins and Harold Lang.

to the dancers. The combination was perfect. Responding to box office demands, Sol Hurok extended The Ballet Theatre's engagement by two weeks, to be followed by a national tour, and the work became a staple item of the company's repertory. Futhermore, Bernstein's conducting fees, combined with performance rights, brought him an income his father could never have dreamed of.

Bernstein's talent seemed to be boundless. Patrons of the New York Philharmonic – who would first have heard of Bernstein as a virtuoso pianist – were still talking about his conducting début and his *Jeremiah* symphony when they were confronted by a smash-hit ballet that revealed a whole new aspect to his skills as a composer – and there was still more to come. Following the enormous success of *Fancy Free*, Oliver Smith suggested to Robbins and Bernstein that they extend and convert the ballet's story into a Broadway musical, to be called *On the Town*.

Various lyricists and writers were mentioned, but Bernstein insisted on Comden and Green. They agreed on the plan in June, but work on the show was to be subjected to a number of delays. Both Bernstein and Adolph Green had to undergo surgery in June (Bernstein for a deviated septum), so they booked themselves in at the same time, which made good publicity copy. As soon as they were well enough, they were joined by Betty Comden, and work on the musical actually began in the hospital. There were to be many more interruptions, however. Bernstein, riding on the crest of his success, had conducting engagements in Montreal, Chicago's Ravinia Festival, and at New York's open-air Lewisohn Stadium (largely thanks to the influence of Koussevitzky). He was reunited with Comden and Green in Los Angeles, where he was to reappear with the Ballet Theatre and also at The Hollywood Bowl (on his twenty-sixth birthday).

Bernstein was a fast-rising star, which meant that he was also becoming national property, involving many public commitments.

Working on *On the Town*, Bernstein with (from left to right) Adolph Green, Betty Comden and Jerome Robbins

He was part of a composers' committee to celebrate Koussevitzky's twentieth year with the Boston Symphony. He appeared at the Metropolitan Opera in a benefit concert for the Anti-Fascist Refugee Committee, where he performed a piano work, *Seven Anniversaries*, dedicated to various friends and family: his sister Shirley, Aaron Copland, William Schuman, Paul Bowles, Alfred Eisner (a friend from Harvard, who had died of cancer), Serge Koussevitzky and Koussevitzky's late wife Natalie. At the request of Yehudi Menuhin and Bruno Walter, Bernstein helped sponsor a new youth orchestra. He was involved in politics, supporting Roosevelt's re-election, was constantly active on behalf of Palestine and conducted a concert to aid Russian war orphans.

In September, Bernstein, Comden and Green returned to New York with what they hoped was a completed show. It was totally different from the original ballet that had inspired its creation, other than that it involved three sailors on leave in New York for twenty-four hours. Comden and Green created a series of complex, often humorous adventures for each of them. Gabey, the sentimental central figure, goes in search of the 'Miss Turnstiles' advertised in the subway in a monthly promotional contest, while his friend Ozzie meets an eccentric lady anthropologist, and Chip – the third member of the trio – finds himself in the clutches of a female taxi driver. Bernstein created a completely new score, consisting of ballads, comedy numbers, interludes and dance music, and used nothing from *Fancy Free*. It was Broadway music at its best and most sophisticated, but far removed from the Coplandesque symphonic jazz score of his ballet.

The producers Oliver Smith and Paul Feigay were having serious problems raising sufficient capital for the production, as they were trying to persuade hardened theatre backers to part with their money for a show created by newcomers without any real Broadway experience. Comden and Green had done a lot of work with The Revuers, but that had been in Greenwich Village and definitely 'off-Broadway'. Jerome Robbins was a talented young dancer and choreographer from a ballet company, and Bernstein was a classical composer-conductor-pianist. After a series of unsuccessful backers' auditions, Smith and Feigay brought in the veteran George Abbott –

one of the most distinguished men of the theatre – to direct the show. Almost immediately they found financial support, including an MGM contract for a film to follow the stage production. (The film, with Gene Kelly, Vera Ellen and Frank Sinatra, became one of the 'legendary' Hollywood musicals, although it changed the original show considerably and removed some of Bernstein's best music.)

Abbott took absolute control and made a number of changes, remoulding and streamlining the production. He reduced a ballet by Robbins, removed one of Bernstein's songs, and re-examined every part of the show with the skill and authority for which he was renowned. For its creators, it was an invaluable experience (just as Bernstein's 'humble' work at Harms-Witmark had trained him in the preparation of sheet music). After an uneasy try-out in Boston, during which Abbott made further drastic alterations (and Bernstein was furiously castigated by Koussevitzky for wasting his time and talent on a musical), *On the Town* opened at the Adelphi Theatre in New York on 28 December 1944.

The reviews were almost unanimously excellent, noting that book, songs and music were beautifully dovetailed, ensuring that the action never lost pace. The *New York Times* drew comparisons with Rodgers and Hammerstein's historic *Oklahoma!*, which had achieved the same integration. Comden and Green, who also appeared in the cast, had made good use of their training in The Revuers, where sophisticated wit and brevity had been synonymous, and Bernstein's masterly score drew praise and recognition from both the popular and the serious press. Once again, he had accepted the challenge of another musical world and emerged triumphant. As a composer, his year had begun with *Jeremiah*, continued with *Fancy Free* and *Seven Anniversaries* for solo piano (some of which would later be incorporated into his *Serenade*, for violin and orchestra), ending with *On the Town*. By any standards, it was an amazing achievement for a young man who had only just established his presence as a conductor.

With so much and such rapid success, Bernstein found himself in almost constant demand. Jerome Robbins was eager to create a second ballet. Oliver Smith talked about another musical with Comden and Green, and Bernstein himself was considering an adaptation of Maxwell Anderson's play *Winterset*, based on the Sacco and Vanzetti

trial, as well as a piano concerto (which was to emerge five years later as his second symphony, *The Age of Anxiety*). In fact, the only work he did compose early in 1945 was *Hashkiveinu*, a short choral prayer for tenor, choir and organ (possibly in memory of his early years with his family at Temple Mishkan Tefila in Roxbury), written for the Park Avenue Synagogue in New York.

In addition, Bernstein was becoming a well-known 'personality', appearing on radio programmes and interviews, and was the subject of articles in glossy magazines such as *Vogue* and *Harper's Bazaar*. He was an ideal guest, being down-to-earth and humorous, witty and erudite, and equally at home discussing jazz or classical music. His image was far removed from that of a Toscanini or a Koussevitzky, who were, to the American public, remote European 'intellectuals', talking a language they did not understand. Meanwhile, Arthur Judson and Bruno Zirato exploited Bernstein's success with guest engagements that in 1945 alone brought him before ten major American orchestras.

His international career might also have commenced that year, when it was announced that a festival would take place in Paris during the summer, directed by Aaron Copland and with Bernstein as chief conductor, to honour American composers and those European composers who had found refuge from the Nazis in America. It was, however, cancelled due to the immediate problems affecting post-war Europe (and possibly also because of artistic and aesthetic differences).

At this point, word of the multi-talented composer-conductor reached Hollywood, nearly always the farthest outpost in the world of the arts at that time. (The distinguished film composer Dimitri Tiomkin insisted that he was originally hired because the producer in question thought he was the composer of Ravel's *Bolero*!) Bernstein was offered the role of music adviser in a 'biopic' about Tchaikovsky, and was even considered for the on-screen role of the composer, with Greta Garbo as Madame von Meck. Another offer proposed a starring role in a film about Rimsky-Korsakov. Fortunately, nothing ever resulted from these extraordinary flirtations with the silver screen, and his only work for Hollywood, apart from the filming of his musicals, was the evocative score composed for Elia Kazan's *On the Waterfront*.

He spent much of April and May of 1945 travelling between New York and Detroit, where he gave six weekly concert broadcasts and, at the end of a hectic spring, took a well-earned holiday in Mexico City, where he met the composer Carlos Chávez and the playwright Tennessee Williams. From there he went on to rent a private villa, with its own pool, in Cuernavaca. As soon as his holiday was over, he was back 'on the road', with guest appearances in San Francisco, Chicago and New York, in Lewisohn Stadium. It should be remembered that air travel was not the normal mode of transport in those days, so that he was criss-crossing the continent exhaustively by train.

Following the acclaim that he enjoyed everywhere he visited, it was clear that Bernstein was ready to lead an orchestra of his own. His musical 'godfather' Serge Koussevitzky came to the rescue, with a letter to Fiorello La Guardia, New York's famous and well-loved mayor, recommending that Bernstein take over the city's other musical organization, the New York City Symphony Orchestra. Also the home of the New York City Ballet, it was housed in the City Center for Music and Dance, a former Mecca Temple, its façade decorated with colourful mosaics, that the city had acquired through a foreclosure. The current director, Leopold Stokowski, had just resigned to take up an appointment at The Hollywood Bowl.

It is more than likely that Koussevitzky made his recommendation because he wanted to see his protégé settle down to the serious business of being a conductor, give up gallivanting round the country like a film star and, above all, turn his back on writing Broadway shows or jazz-oriented music, which he did not understand, and both of which he despised and considered undignified for a true *maestro* in the great European tradition. Already seventy-one, Koussevitzky probably saw Bernstein as his eventual successor in Boston, and wanted him well-prepared for the task.

Bernstein was formally offered the post on his twenty-seventh birthday – 25 August 1945. He always placed great emphasis on certain dates in his life. Rodzinski had offered him the New York Philharmonic appointment on his twenty-fifth birthday. His surprise début with that orchestra had taken place on 14 November 1944, seven years to the day that he had accidentally met Aaron Copland in a New York theatre.

Bernstein, now a familiar name in musical circles, is given a suitably 'glamorous' treatment by the photographer Baron.

His new season at City Center did not begin until October, but there was much to be done before then. The orchestra's career had been sketchy and it had very little musical identity when compared with the New York Philharmonic, two blocks away at Carnegie Hall. Furthermore, its personnel had long needed an injection of new blood. For years it had survived rather than flourished.

But Bernstein was always full of innovative musical ideas. He was already championing the work of fellow American composers whenever the opportunity arose. (Even in his Harvard days, he had written of developing an American national musical style that would complement its European ancestry by adding jazz and Latin-American influences.) Furthermore, the war ended in August and there would be a huge influx of talented ex-service musicians looking for peacetime employment.

Whether by good fortune or by design, or because the gods smile on those destined for greatness, Leonard Bernstein was once again in the right place at the right time.

2

Bernstein departing from La
Guardia airport with his sister
Shirley, 21 June 1947

*His spirit is contagious. The compelling power
that radiates from the podium and galvanises
one in front of the television is real. He can say
it is raining outside and make one want to go
outside and stand in it.*

Schuyler Chapin, in
Musical Chairs – A Life in the Arts

The Road to Stardom 1945–57

Leonard Bernstein's amazing run of successes seemed to fill him with additional energy, and the autumn of 1945 marked the start of a whirlwind existence that he would pursue for the rest of his life. He plunged into the business of establishing an all-new City Symphony orchestra, with exhaustive auditions for countless young aspirants. Places were hotly contested and he replaced half the members of Stokowski's former orchestra, employing musicians of an average age of thirty. The season running from October 1945 to April 1946 was to feature twelve pairs of concerts on Mondays and Tuesdays (the latter starting early enough to attract commuters before they left for the suburbs). His programming was eclectic, imaginative and ambitious and would include, in addition to some standard repertoire items, works by Copland, Britten, Shostakovich, Stravinsky, Hindemith, Milhaud, Diamond, Chávez, Bartók and Blitzstein, whose *Airborne Symphony* would be narrated by Orson Welles.

Despite his ever-demanding schedule, he always found time to maintain a regular correspondence with family and friends, particularly Aaron Copland who, while he unstintingly offered generous help and support, seemed to hesitate in his total admiration of Bernstein as a composer. Copland was also his confidant when it came to his private hopes and aspirations, as well as his (fairly constant) amatory exploits, all of them homosexual. In letters and postcards from his travels around America, Bernstein delighted in keeping Helen Coates fully informed of his musical triumphs and Aaron Copland of his career dreams and 'conquests'. Copland, whose own private life was always discreetly veiled, frequently expressed disapproval of his friend's indiscretions and self-indulgences.

From his early twenties onwards Bernstein regularly sought the advice of various 'shrinks' and it is usually assumed that he was troubled over his sexual identity. Despite his gay lifestyle, he clearly enjoyed the company of women and talked of a future in which, like his idol Koussevitzky, he would settle down as a good family man. (He often expressed contempt for effeminate 'queens'.) It is more than likely that he was equally worried about his future career. He understood the danger of being a jack-of-all-trades but, for the moment anyway, he was faced with the dilemma of appearing to be master of them all. Many times throughout his life he would announce that he was going to give up conducting and dedicate himself to composing. In later years, he probably saw himself as a latter-day Gustav Mahler, the composer-conductor with whom Bernstein is often identified, who escaped to compose in the peace and solitude of the countryside once his season's obligations had been fulfilled. In a modern age dominated by communications and constantly filled with attractive new offers, it was less easy for Bernstein to refuse his admirers. But in 1945, as soon as he had emerged as a versatile composer, self-evidently fluent in many styles, he told *PM* magazine that he saw himself primarily as a conductor. With his own orchestra to direct, an exciting season about to begin and with Koussevitzky in Boston urging him to establish his conducting 'roots', it is easy to understand why he made such a statement.

His first season was a resounding success. Olin Downes wrote of Bernstein's 'exceptional brilliancy', adding that the orchestra had improved noticeably since the previous season under Stokowski. The *Brooklyn Eagle* observed that Bernstein 'created a kind of white heat'. This praise did not pass unnoticed by the New York Philharmonic or Artur Rodzinski. Understandably, Bernstein was not invited back to Carnegie Hall as a guest conductor. His presence at City Center, however, gave New York concert-goers an added bonus. Rodzinski, not to be outdone, came up with exciting programmes of his own and everyone benefited from the musical rivalry between the two organizations.

Despite his new achievements, Bernstein had his critics. Olin Downes of the *New York Times* had been a constant champion of Bernstein, from his New York Philharmonic début onwards, although even he confessed that Bernstein's emotional and quasi-choreographic conducting style did not always seem essential to his music-making. Virgil Thomson, writing in the *New York Herald-Tribune*, was openly hostile, complaining of Bernstein's Hollywood leanings, his theatrical facial expressions, his exaggerated body movements and his distortions

Artur Rodzinski, musical director of the New York Philharmonic, who gave Bernstein his first important appointment as assistant conductor of the orchestra

of the music. For his part, Bernstein dismissed such attacks as a personal vendetta in response to his rejection of Thomson both as a lover and as a composer whose music he had refused to programme. Even at this early stage of his career, Bernstein was the subject of strongly opposing points of view.

One other event, early in 1946, was to be of lifelong significance. Following a concert performance with the distinguished Chilean pianist Claudio Arrau, Bernstein went to a reception at which he met an attractive young compatriot of Arrau's, the actress Felicia Montealegre y Cohn. Of mixed ancestry (her father, an American mining engineer, was the grandson of a rabbi, and her mother, a Costa Rican Catholic, had moved with him to Chile when Felicia was a baby), she had opted for American citizenship and settled in the United States. She was working in an actor's studio in New York, and continuing piano studies under Arrau's guidance. According to friends, she had seen Bernstein conduct at City Center and had decided there and then that she would marry him, even before they had met. Those who were present at the dinner are convinced that it was 'love at first sight' for them both. Even though their engagement – announced at the end of that year – would be broken off, and Bernstein's constant travels brought about months of enforced separation, Felicia Montealegre (she dropped the 'Cohn' from her father for her stage career) eventually did become his wife and mother of their three children.

In May of 1946, Bernstein made his European début, at the first Prague Spring Festival in Czechoslovakia. On the way home, he visited Paris where he met Nadia Boulanger, whose many students had included Jean Françaix and Lennox Berkeley, as well as – much closer to Bernstein's heart – Walter Piston and Aaron Copland. In June he flew back to London where he appeared with the London Philharmonic. He received mixed reviews from the press, who were somewhat startled by his conducting style: a highly charged, athletic performance, in which Bernstein at times seemed not only to direct the orchestra, but also to choreograph the music and perform an interpretative dance for the audience. His face, when visible, displayed a wide range of emotional reactions (presumably for the players), and his extravagant body language could involve anything from a sexy 1920s 'shimmy' to a three-foot leap in the air, timed to coincide with a dramatic downbeat. (He once said of himself, 'I'm the only person I know who's paid to have a fit in public!') He was surprised by the cool reception of his performances and perhaps missed some of the star treatment to which he had already become accustomed in America. He also suffered the discomforts of bad weather, a flu attack, poor food and the inadequate facilities of post-war Britain. He visited Benjamin Britten at Glyndebourne, recorded the Ravel Piano Concerto in London, conducted a gala *Fancy Free* for the visiting Ballet Theatre at the Royal Opera House, then rushed back to Tanglewood, where he was Koussevitzky's assistant in conducting classes, to begin exhaustive rehearsals of Britten's opera *Peter Grimes*.

Tanglewood consisted mostly of talented students and was ill-prepared to take on a work of such size and complexity in the five weeks that had been allotted to it, but Bernstein accepted the challenge and transmitted his enthusiasm to the entire company. The opera was admired, but the production was given a mixed reception. Britten came to the final week of rehearsals, and Koussevitzky (who had commissioned and who was very proud of 'Peter und Grimes', as he called it) was dismayed to find that the opera's composer was, like Copland and Diamond – and maybe also his beloved 'Lenyushka' – a 'pederast', as he rather quaintly identified homosexuals. Britten was clearly unimpressed, dismissing the production as a 'very lively student performance', and although Bernstein championed his music over the years, he was never invited to take part in Britten's Aldeburgh Festival.

Directly after *Peter Grimes*, Bernstein was joined by Jerome Robbins to work on a new commission from the Ballet Theatre, to be called *Facsimile*. The plot line, developed by Robbins, is simple and with dark undertones, in sharp contrast to the basically optimistic and satirical *Fancy Free*. Taking as its theme the desperate search of people seeking a meaningful relationship only to find themselves with a facsimile of the real thing, the plot involves three dancers – two men and a woman – on an empty beach. The woman is joined by the first man, with whom she carries on a flirtation leading to a moment of passion, but the artificiality of their feelings causes them to withdraw from one another. The second man joins them and, after an initial period of teasing in which she plays one man off against the other, the woman finds herself in an increasingly cruel romantic triangle. Eventually she is physically thrown from one to the other until she cries 'Stop!' In the silence that follows, only her sobbing is heard and the men stand aside. Embarrassed, the men depart, leaving the woman alone and unfulfilled. In his own programme note to the ballet, Bernstein explains that the characters cannot find a true connection with each other, '... because they are unintegrated personalities with little if any capacity for real relations.'

Needless to say, Bernstein's would-be analysts have read much into this statement, asking whether it is a reflection of his own sexual duality and uncertainty of commitment. Whatever the case, *Facsimile* received mixed reviews. The dancers, particularly Norah Kaye, were praised, as was Oliver Smith's set, and Jerome Robbins (to whom the score was dedicated) was accorded respectful praise for an intriguing psychological study; the ballet as a whole, however, was anticlimactic after the ebullient *Fancy Free* and within five years it had been dropped from the repertory of the Ballet Theatre.

Bernstein's score picks up the musical thread where *Fancy Free* left off, but it is a noticeably more sophisticated work of great lyricism, with a strongly rhythmic but less overtly jazz-orientated drive. It was probably his finest and most characteristic composition to date. *Choreographic Essay*, Bernstein's brilliant adaptation of the score for concert performance, was given its première six months later with the Rochester Philharmonic. It is surprising that both the ballet and the concert version have been overlooked in recent years.

Towards the end of the year, Hollywood beckoned yet again and Bernstein travelled to the West Coast for meetings with the producer Lester Cowan, who wanted him to compose a score, write the screenplay and even star in a film adapted from a novel called *The Beckoning Fair One* by the English thriller-writer, Oliver Onions. Like all Hollywood projects, it would carry a handsome fee, which also appealed to Bernstein. Although *On the Town* had earned him a sizeable income, none of his 'serious' works had been taken up in the concert world and neither Mitropoulos nor Koussevitzky had performed any of them. Bernstein stayed at Cowan's ranch in the San Fernando Valley, travelling there with Felicia Montealegre, who had been his regular companion whenever they were both in New York. A contract was agreed with Cowan, and, to Koussevitzky's relief and with the cautious approval of the Bernstein family, Leonard announced that he and Felicia were engaged.

Bernstein left Hollywood to fulfil his next series of concert engagements, but Felicia remained there, looking for screen work, and for the moment, she dropped out of Bernstein's life. He was due to appear over three weeks with the Boston Symphony Orchestra, conducting in both Boston and New York and, although Koussevitzky was delighted with the news of his engagement, he took exception to his protégé's inclusion of the concert version of *Facsimile* in his programme, considering it unworthy and insisted on its removal. (Directly afterwards, Bernstein was scheduled for a three-week tour with the Rochester Symphony, which did perform it.)

An orchestra's concert plans are made anything up to eighteen months ahead of the date (if nothing else, to ensure that soloists reserve their time), so while Bernstein still had one further season with the New York City Symphony, he was already on the lookout for a bigger and better-funded organization. He had hopes for the Rochester orchestra, but they had just selected Erich Leinsdorf on the assumption that Bernstein would probably inherit Boston. Early in 1947, magazines had begun speculating on which conductor would replace Koussevitzky when he retired and the maestro had always hoped that Bernstein would be his successor – but both he and his protégé misjudged the conservative attitude of Boston's controlling establishment.

In Europe, the United States has always given the impression of being a single, united country in its mores and attitudes, but in 1947, Boston (geographically farther from New York than London is from Paris) was philosophically and socially even further removed from New York, let alone Los Angeles, than one would imagine. 'Banned in Boston' had traditionally been an enticing inducement to encourage sales of a racy book or a sexy new film (and, in fact, an erotic kiss in the Boston run of *Facsimile* had been removed by order of the city fathers). In such an environment, Bernstein's family background, his religion and his Broadway and jazz affiliations weighed heavily against him as a suitable replacement for Koussevitzky, and recent events had only served to confirm such negative opinions. Even worse was the news that the would-be conductor of the staid Boston Symphony, despite his denials, had signed a contract to become a film star.

In a recent biography of Mitropoulos (*Priest of Music* by William Trotter, who completed work originally undertaken by the late Oliver Daniel), there is a very strange story that suggests that Bernstein, ever a self-proclaimed disciple of the conductor, betrayed the man who had sponsored his career (and had even supported him financially at Curtis), when he believed that they were both competing for the Boston Symphony. Various interviews imply that Bernstein, knowing Koussevitzky's homophobia, warned him that Mitropoulos was gay and an unsuitable successor. Another version of the story is even more sinister and claims that Koussevitzky, disliking the Greek conductor for reasons little beyond petty jealousy, conspired with his protégé to denounce Mitropoulos to the orchestra's board. The board, however, appointed Charles Munch, despite Koussevitzky's championship of Bernstein.

What makes either story difficult to credit is that, whatever his hopes and any arrogant self-assessment, Bernstein would have been a non-starter in the Boston Symphony stakes, and should have realized it, even with Koussevitzky's somewhat naïve support. The position of Music Director in an American orchestra carries many social as well as musical responsiblities. As a local boy from not-quite-the-right side of the tracks, with a Broadway hit and showbiz associates – even worse, a Jew! – Bernstein would never have met the appropriate criteria in class-conscious Boston, no matter the extent of his successes elsewhere. (At one time he had even been advised to change his name to make it more acceptable to such a WASP-dominated community.) And Koussevitzky, who was aware of the generally relaxed sexual mores at Tanglewood, had now more than a suspicion that Bernstein himself had been a practising homosexual for some years, despite his recent engagement to Felicia.

Later, in 1957, when Bernstein first came to share the New York Philharmonic with Mitropoulos, he was critical of the orchestra's lack of discipline under the older man, but it should be remembered that, in musical matters, he wrote and spoke with a conviction, and sometimes a lack of tact, that was almost Jesuitical in its zeal. (In later years, Felicia talked of his 'foot in mouth' disease!) Also, following press attacks on the Philharmonic, Bernstein was ambitious enough to cast himself as the architect of the orchestra's reconstruction. But Bernstein was a constant and vocal admirer of Mitropoulos all his life, far longer than would have been necessary had it not been heartfelt. Whenever he conducted, he wore a cross that had once belonged to Mitropoulos – as a good luck token, or possibly for deeper reasons; he was a very superstitious man. (After Koussevitzky's death, he always conducted wearing a pair of the maestro's cuff-links, which he would kiss before going on-stage.) It is therefore hard to believe that, when Boston sought a new conductor, Bernstein would have stabbed his musical idol in the back quite so ruthlessly. Even some years after his death, he still seems to inspire love/hate emotional responses in people's memories.

Whatever his frustrations in finding a future orchestral 'home' might have been in 1947, nothing could match the excitement and the joy of travelling (with his family, but not including Felicia) to Palestine in April of that year. For centuries, 'Next year in Jerusalem!', the final words of the Passover service, had been shared by Jews everywhere, dreaming of a time when they would have a homeland of their own, and in the city of Jerusalem Bernstein experienced the thrill of conducting the Palestine Philharmonic Orchestra in his own *Jeremiah*. His audiences throughout the tour treated him like a pop star, taking enormous national pride in the young Jewish maestro who was already conquering America. At that time, the country was torn apart by political conflict, with opposing parties striving for independence either through negotiation, terrorism or open war, and Bernstein willingly identified himself as a part of their cause. He rehearsed amid explosions, risked everyday dangers and gave concerts in cinemas, makeshift halls and before a huge audience in the open air at a *kibbutz*. Compared with its American counterparts, the orchestra was second or even third class, but the players adored Bernstein, responding with greater skill than they had displayed since their opening concerts with Arturo Toscanini. By early June, after the Bernstein entourage had left, the Board formally offered him the post of Musical Director, which he set aside, asking only to be 'musical adviser' and promising long-lasting support. His New York management saw no great advantage in his association with Palestine and were still angling to find him an American orchestra. In addition, Koussevitzky continued to promote his cause in Boston. Bernstein completed the rest of his tour, conducting the European première of

A reception in Jerusalem, Palestine, where Bernstein was fêted wherever he went. On his left is Golda Meir, Zionist Women's leader, who would later become Prime Minister of Israel.

An Arab rifleman dashes from a church in Jerusalem during the war of independence.

Copland's Third Symphony in Prague, *Jeremiah* in Paris and further concerts in Brussels and The Hague.

Back in America, there were concerts with the New York Philharmonic at Lewisohn Stadium, followed by a new Tanglewood season, for which he composed a humorous short *Fanfare for Bima* in honour of Koussevitzky's seventy-third birthday (Bima being the maestro's dog). He conducted the Boston Symphony and also recorded some chamber works by Stravinsky with members of the orchestra.

Later, he was joined by Felicia, who clearly found life amid the Bernstein clan something of a strain. Despite earlier conflicts with his father, Bernstein was deeply attached to his family and tried whenever possible to share important religious occasions with them. He remained devoted to his mother, but was perhaps closest to his sister Shirley, who had taken part in his musical activities since early childhood, starring in some of his Sharon productions. (At Harvard, she had been in *The Cradle Will Rock*. In *Fancy Free*, the ballet opens with the sound of a blues song playing on a juke-box, for which she recorded the voice, and she was in the chorus of *On the Town*.)

In mid August, Felicia went back to New York. Bernstein
accompanied her, then returned to Tanglewood, where he spent much
of his time with the jazz pianist John Mehegan. In September, New
York gossip columnists claimed that his engagement to Felicia had
been broken off. In fact, he saw Felicia occasionally in the autumn
months and it was she who finally suggested in December that they
should call off any wedding plans.

Bernstein's third and last season with the New York City
Symphony opened with his first performance of a Mahler symphony
(No. 2, the 'Resurrection'). At that time, some of the New York
reviewers were highly critical of the music, finding it overblown and
'empty'. Mahler had always predicted, 'My time will come.' Various
conductors, recognizing his greatness, had performed his music over
the years. These included Klemperer, Mitropoulos and, of course,
Bruno Walter, who had been a friend and student of the composer.
Their efforts, like Bernstein's, had mostly met with critical apathy and
half-empty houses. It would still take some years, together with
persistent programming (particularly by Bernstein), for Mahler's
prediction to come true.

It was a shorter season than the previous two, still plagued by lack
of sufficient funding from the City of New York, and one in which
Bernstein's critics noted that the playing seemed to lack the quality
and discipline it had shown before. But Bernstein was congratulated
for his imaginative programming and even Virgil Thomson, still
unhappy with the conductor's style, had to concede that he had
created an interesting survey of the twentieth century's music and had
also developed a new audience for it.

The final showpiece of his season was a staged performance of *The
Cradle Will Rock*. The presentation was so successful that it was moved
to a Broadway theatre for a limited engagement and Bernstein
conducted its first three performances between Christmas and the
New Year. Conducting engagements in Minnesota and Texas
followed, after which he again performed Mahler's Symphony No. 2
in Boston, this time much more favourably received.

At this point, early in 1948, his career seemed to be in a state of
suspended animation. He would not continue with the New York
City Symphony and, although Judson and Zirato could guarantee a
number of guest engagements, Bernstein needed an important

orchestra of his own. Boston remained a possibility, however remote, and Koussevitzky was doing his best to help, but the Board's decision would not be known until April.

After his Boston concerts, Bernstein was supposed to have made a second visit to his beloved Palestine, but he cancelled it, at first citing concern that as an American and a Jew he would be an obvious target for Arab terrorists. Later, he formally cancelled the visit because of 'doctors orders ... for a period of complete rest'. The orchestra was distressed by his decision, fearing that other guest musicians might follow suit and avoid their war-torn country, but Bernstein remained in the United States. It is unlikely that he avoided the trip out of fear for his personal safety, as he was deeply emotionally involved in the creation of a Jewish state and on his previous visit had revelled in occasional brushes with danger. The medical reasons for his absence were never revealed, and Bernstein enjoyed a brief respite from public life.

In the spring of 1948, Bernstein changed publishers, moving to G. Schirmer, who listed a number of works by him: four more *Anniversaries* for solo piano, dedicated to Helen Coates, the composer David Diamond, John Mehegan and Felicia Montealegre; *La Bonne Cuisine*, consisting of four sung recipes, dedicated to Jennie Tourel; and a set of brass pieces, dedicated to various dogs (including the *Fanfare for Bima* that he had written for Koussevitzky). The most important item, however, was his Second Symphony, subtitled *The Age of Anxiety* and based on a long poem by W. H. Auden, on which he may have begun preliminary work, but which was a long way from completion.

When the Boston Symphony finally announced that Koussevitzky's replacement would be Charles Munch, Bernstein seemed prepared for the disappointment. Koussevitzky had even threatened to resign if Bernstein was not chosen as his successor but, to his surprise, the Board, whose patrician members did not bow to such pressures, had politely accepted his resignation. Meanwhile, Bernstein had reconsidered the offer from Palestine and had accepted the post of Artistic Director (later changing back to the lesser Music Adviser), starting in September. From the beginning, he had been inspired by his contact with the Jewish state and his own contribution would be to build a great new orchestra. Without belittling his altruism too

ungraciously, it is also probable that he saw no full-time American
orchestras on his personal horizon for at least the next year or so.
Shortly after, he left for another European tour, which would take him
to Budapest, Milan, Munich and, for the first time, Vienna – with the
city's Symphony Orchestra. The Vienna Philharmonic was yet to come.

On his return to America in the summer, Bernstein served again at
Tanglewood, teaching conducting students and giving two concerts
with the Boston Symphony Orchestra, but he was eager to continue
work on *The Age of Anxiety*, and left almost immediately for Taos,
New Mexico, accompanied by his brother, Burton Bernstein, who
shared the long drive, and by the poet Stephen Spender. By September
he was in Palestine, already self-proclaimed as Israel, to take up his
post with the renamed Israel Philharmonic Orchestra.

He spent two months in the country, giving forty concerts in sixty
days and living a quasi-military existence amid the people's struggle
for independence, contributing to their efforts and witnessing the
suffering as well as the victories. His work was physically and mentally
exhausting, leaving little time for composition, although he completed
the *Dirge* that opens the second part of his *Age of Anxiety*. A deadline
had been set for the symphony, which would be presented at the
Boston Symphony's spring season, less than six months ahead and
with many scheduled engagements (in Rome, Boston, Philadelphia,
New York, Buffalo and Pittsburgh, including a tour with the
Pittsburgh Symphony) to be undertaken before that date. When he
left Israel at the end of a triumphant and deeply moving stay, he was
again offered the post of Musical Director, but set it aside because of
all his other commitments.

The Age of Anxiety, dedicated to Koussevitzky, was first performed
on 8 April 1949 by the Boston Symphony, directed by Koussevitzky
and with Bernstein performing the solo piano part. The work had
taken him nearly two years to complete and, according to Bernstein's
original programme note, had been written '... in Taos, in
Philadelphia, in Richmond Mass., in Tel Aviv, in planes, in hotel
lobbies, and finally (the week preceding the première) in Boston ...'.
Formally titled Symphony No. 2, it is in fact more of a piano
concerto. Bernstein saw the solo piano as representing himself as a
witness to the subject matter inspired by Auden's very long Pulitzer-
Prize-winning poem from which the symphony takes its subtitle. He

An open-air concert by the walls of Beersheba – Bernstein and the renamed Israel Philharmonic perform Gershwin's *Rhapsody in Blue*, October 1948.

added that it was not a concerto in the virtuoso image that such a title suggests, although the solo piano part does require a virtuoso technique.

Over the years, Bernstein's appraisal of parts of his symphony changed. Initially he had been so deeply impressed by Auden's poem, which is about the search for faith in a contemporary world, that he had composed music inspired by the descriptions he had encountered on the printed page. It was never intended as programme music, but he claimed that he had discovered that certain programmatic effects had, in his words, 'written themselves' subconsciously into the music. For example, he had scored a celesta to be struck four times, suggesting the striking of a clock, at a moment in the (musical) work when Auden's (literary) characters find themselves together in the early hours of the morning. Much of the poem concerns three men and a girl in a New York bar, engaged in a 'symposium on the stages of man'. (Bernstein liked the framework of a symposium, and later used it for his violin *Serenade*, somewhat eruditely subtitled *After Plato's 'Symposium'.*)

The work is divided into two Parts. There is a short *Prologue*, introducing the four characters, followed by *The Seven Ages* (a set of variations), in which man's life is evaluated from the four characters'

Jerome Robbins (second from right) rehearsing the ballet performed to the score of *Age of Anxiety*. The première of the ballet took place on the same evening as the first performance of the symphony in New York. Unfortunately, Auden's poetic images proved difficult to reproduce in choreographic form.

In his apartment in Carnegie Hall Bernstein adds a new souvenir to his growing collection – the poster of his first performance with the Palestine Philharmonic Orchestra.

points of view; then *Seven Stages* (further variations), a dream-like episode in which the characters exchange partners in various combinations. The music presents a lyrical, somewhat Brahmsian piano concerto, updated to the middle of the twentieth century, with sombre colours and moments of quiet reflection, although a listener will not be particularly conscious of the variation forms that Bernstein employs. Part Two opens with a *Dirge*, during which the four people, in a cab bound for the girl's apartment, mourn the loss of a universal father-figure to guide and protect them. Bernstein describes the *Dirge* as employing in a harmonic way a twelve-tone row, from which the main theme evolves; the contrasting middle section is of 'almost Brahmsian romanticism'. While the composer refers to the tone row, a device in serial music, the work is not serially conceived. In other words, Bernstein's theme is created from the twelve notes of the octave (including the black notes) without repeating those already played. This is followed by the *Masque*, a jazz interlude for piano and percussion, suggesting the characters' efforts to celebrate, which ends in anti-climax and (in Bernstein's words) 'the dispersal of the actors'. Finally, there is the *Epilogue* which, for Bernstein, represents faith itself. In the original version of the symphony, the piano (that is, composer) played no role, as if watching a film on a screen, with a certain mockery of faith that Bernstein felt represented Auden's rather sombre detachment.

Bernstein later rewrote the finale, adding a piano cadenza before the coda to round out the instrument's concert function. As a musician, he could see that its exclusion from the finale detracted from the structure of the work. In addition, he conceded that when he first undertook the symphony, he considered it essential that the listener should have read Auden's poem. Later he accepted that the music had acquired a life – and a personality – of its own.

In effect, Bernstein was summing up the theme he later presented on television: that music isn't *about* anything. Auden's poem may have inspired Bernstein to write *The Age of Anxiety* and, in his mind, Bernstein may have followed the sequence of Auden's text, but he

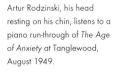

Artur Rodzinski, his head resting on his chin, listens to a piano run-through of *The Age of Anxiety* at Tanglewood, August 1949.

created a living, structured work of art which requires no explanation or 'programme'. Indeed, few concert-goers are likely to have read Auden's poem, and even Auden himself, who did not appear to reciprocate Bernstein's admiration for him, recognized little of his writing in the music, adding that any connections were 'rather distant'.

The work was enthusiastically received in Boston and even Koussevitzky, with his contempt for what he called 'jezz', accepted the music of the *Masque* sequence. A year later, after a New York Philharmonic performance conducted by Bernstein, with his friend Lukas Foss playing the piano part, the reviews were more guarded. Olin Downes, forever Bernstein's supporter, used the phrase 'a triumph of superficiality' for the *Epilogue*, but added kindly that it expressed the anxiety of modern life.

The Age of Anxiety, whatever its original inspiration, was Bernstein's most ambitious creation during the first part of his career. It contains

Bernstein with W. H. Auden, whose book-length poem *The Age of Anxiety* inspired Bernstein's Second Symphony

a number of Bernstein 'trademarks': his use of jazz, a finale which expresses a universal human optimism and, above all, a sense of theatre. In his own programme note, Bernstein wrote that he was willing to plead guilty to a charge of 'theatricality', adding that he suspected that every work he wrote, no matter the medium, was really music for the theatre. The New York première was given at Carnegie Hall in the afternoon and, on the same evening, a new ballet, choreographed by Jerome Robbins, was danced to the same score.

The symphony has been performed internationally by many interpreters and will in all probability continue in concert repertory long after the lengthy poem that inspired it has disappeared from the shelves of bookshops. It is a major contribution to the symphonic repertoire of the twentieth century, composed at a time when most musicians believed that the symphony was already an outmoded form.

The rest of Bernstein's spring was taken up with adapting some of his music for the MGM film of *On the Town*. To his disappointment, Hollywood remained an editorial law unto itself and the changes made were more ruthless than George Abbott's original improvements to the stage version. The haunting song 'Lonely Town', one of Bernstein's most beautiful, was taken out, and the ballet music from the second act of the stage show drastically reduced and changed to fit Gene Kelly's choreography. The film, nevertheless, proved to be one of MGM's finest productions, an indicator that the Hollywood professionals realized the great differences between sophisticated New York theatre-goers and international audiences.

Conducting engagements followed, including a concert version of Wagner's *Tristan und Isolde,* and Bernstein again served under Koussevitzky at Tanglewood's summer school, once more performing *The Age of Anxiety*. In the autumn months, he returned to composing, working on two projects: a jazz piece for the bandleader Woody Herman, and incidental music for a new production of J. M. Barrie's children's favourite, *Peter Pan*, which would star Jean Arthur and Boris Karloff. Before completing them, however, he had further concerts, including the world première of Olivier Messiaen's huge and magnificent *Turangalîla Symphony*, a Koussevitzky Foundation commission which, with one or two notable exceptions, failed to impress American critics in its early performances. Soon after, Bernstein left for Key West in Florida, to complete the songs, choruses

Following page, Frank Sinatra, Jules Munshin and Gene Kelly in the film version of On the Town (1949)

and incidental music for *Peter Pan*, which opened in New York in April 1950, by which time Bernstein had already travelled to Italy and on to Israel. But before leaving the United States he signed a contract with Columbia Records, a division of CBS, which was to be renewed in 1956 and again in 1959 (to give him virtually *carte blanche* to record whatever repertoire he chose). Over the next twenty-five years he would create one of the largest recorded catalogues of any artist, surpassed in size only by that of Herbert von Karajan.

In Israel, as *Jeremiah* had been his calling-card on his first visit, *The Age of Anxiety* became his latest showpiece, and he gave ten performances of it, conducting them from the piano. (His first experience of pianist-conductors had been as a teenager, when he had been astonished by the skill with which Mitropoulos could direct an orchestra from the keyboard.)

During the period of their separation, Felicia Montealegre's career had also blossomed, both on the stage and in the new medium of television. After breaking off her engagement to Bernstein, she had mostly dedicated herself to her work, but had found a new companion in the actor Richard Hart, with whom she was living in 1950. Hart, who was already married, was an alcoholic and sometimes violent, but Felicia was devoted to him. She remained, however, very much in Bernstein's thoughts and, even while he was in Israel, his correspondence with his sister Shirley indicated that he hoped that he would one day be reunited with Felicia, whom he saw not only as a future partner but also as a defence against what he often described as 'the demon' of his homosexual inclinations.

When Bernstein returned to the United States in the summer of 1950, he made some effort at a reconciliation with Felicia, but she was not prepared to leave Hart or, for that matter, to sacrifice her career for Bernstein. She complained that Helen Coates had always disapproved both of her and of their engagement. Bernstein, perhaps hoping to mollify Felicia, sacked 'Miss Coates', but almost immediately rehired her, realizing that she was probably more indispensable to the management of his life than a wife would be.

Bernstein attended a somewhat changed Tanglewood, over which Koussevitzky, in anticipation of the arrival of Munch in Boston, was no longer in total command. Bernstein returned to Europe shortly afterwards, this time accompanied by his sister and brother, for

Bernstein rehearsing
at New York's open-air
Lewisohn Stadium, c. 1949

appearances in France, at the Edinburgh Festival, his début with the
Concertgebouw Orchestra in Amsterdam, and an extended holiday
with his sister that started in Eire and continued to the south of
France, Spain and the island of Majorca.

As well as keeping her brother informed about Felicia's developing
career, Shirley Bernstein maintained contact with Felicia throughout
the period of her estrangement from Leonard. When Shirley and
Leonard returned from their holiday by sea to New York, they were
greeted at the docks by Felicia. While the three were having a
celebratory drink, the news came that Richard Hart had collapsed in
a Third Avenue bar. Felicia was with him at the hospital when he

died later the same day, and Bernstein was there to comfort and console her. He was about to embark on a long itinerary of concert appearances, but took time to see her whenever he was back in New York.

The year 1951 started out with exhaustive conducting engagements, beginning with a heavy tour to raise funds for the visiting Israel Philharmonic. The tour was to be shared with Koussevitzky but the maestro fell ill, placing the greater burden on Bernstein and two colleagues. The orchestra was mostly well received and, because the tour was extended, Bernstein occasionally took leave to fulfil other engagements, including the world première of Charles Ives's Second Symphony with the New York Philharmonic, and appearances with the Chicago Symphony.

It was Bernstein's intention to give up conducting at the end of the tour and dedicate himself to composing for several years. Shortly after the Israel Philharmonic returned home, however, Bernstein travelled to Koussevitzky's winter ranch in Arizona, ostensibly to discuss plans as far ahead as 1953, only to realize that the maestro was more concerned with the future of Tanglewood should he become too ill to continue there. Bernstein's final engagement for the first half of the year was in Mexico City, and he moved from there to Cuernavaca, inviting himself to the home of Ernest Hemingway's ex-wife, Martha Gellhorn, where he began work on his one-act opera, *Trouble in Tahiti*. He advised everyone in New York that he would not accept further conducting engagements. He composed steadily through the month of May and would happily have continued, but a phone call summoned him to Boston. Koussevitzky, whose health was deteriorating rapidly, was deeply concerned about Tanglewood, fearing that he would no longer be able to supervise. Bernstein returned in time to spend a few hours with him, making plans for the future, but his guide and mentor died on 4 June 1951.

Tanglewood was due to start in a few weeks, but Charles Munch was conducting in Europe, Aaron Copland, the deputy Director, was in Rome, so it was left to Bernstein to take over the conducting studies and some of the administrative duties. Even more important was the responsibility of continuing the benevolent tradition that Koussevitzky had created. The maestro had been a teacher and an inspiration to countless young musicians and a father-figure to

Bernstein throughout his formative years. He was determined that his great institution should be maintained.

During the festival, Felicia Montealegre returned from a European trip and travelled immediately to Tanglewood, where she and Bernstein again discussed marriage. This time they avoided a lengthy engagement process, and the day after the final Tanglewood concert Olga Koussevitzky, widow of the conductor, made the announcement. Felicia converted fully to Judaism before the wedding, which took place less than a month later in Temple Mishkan Tefilah in Roxbury, where Bernstein had worshipped during his childhood years. They left by car for their honeymoon, driving to Cuernavaca, where Bernstein would continue his sabbatical and hoped to finish his opera. (The conductor Antonio de Almeida, a family friend who was living there, recalled that Felicia developed a sudden desire for an English afternoon tea, complete with silver service, razor-thin cucumber sandwiches and dainty cakes. He explained that such things were not usually available in Mexico, but eventually found somewhere that could cater to her whim. When Felicia called de Almeida to thank him, asking for the address, she was delighted to learn that it had been the local brothel!) Their stay lasted only three months. Bernstein received an urgent call to replace Munch in Boston, and Felicia was offered various television roles. In addition, they were expecting their first child.

After Boston, Bernstein's next major engagement was as visiting professor at Brandeis University, outside Boston, where he would direct a new Festival of Creative Arts. *Trouble in Tahiti* would be presented and, in order to complete the work, he went to Yaddo, an artist's colony in upstate New York, leaving Felicia in New York. The festival offered an exciting programme, involving jazz, poetry readings, art exhibits and documentary films. It also featured the first performance of Blitzstein's new translation of Kurt Weill's *The Threepenny Opera* and a concert dedicated to the memory of Koussevitzky. Bernstein's opera was performed in an open-air theatre on the first night of the festival, but was not very well received due to the uncomfortable circumstances of the late hour, poor amplification and extraneous noises. At that time, Bernstein was still refusing conducting engagements to concentrate on his work as a composer. Tanglewood was to start soon, and he set about rewriting the finale of

Trouble in Tahiti, with which he was dissatisfied. The new version was presented during the Tanglewood Festival.

Trouble in Tahiti, whose basic theme – not unlike the ballet *Facsimile* – is our failure to communicate meaningfully with one other, is presented in a bitingly satirical style. The central characters, embarrassingly named Sam and Dinah (those of his father and paternal grandmother), are depicted in an idealized 'television-land' home. They are accompanied by a vocal close-harmony trio which, rather like a Greek chorus, comments on the glories of American suburban living. Sam and Dinah give the appearance of a successful, happy young couple, but their life is a sham. In *Trouble in Tahiti* we see a typical day. Sam cannot spare the time to watch their son Junior (whom we do not meet) in a school play because he is taking part in a handball competition. Dinah visits her psychiatrist. Sam is at the gym and Dinah goes to the cinema, where she sees a dreadful technicolour tropical romance entitled *Trouble in Tahiti*. Afterwards she treats herself to a new hat and, while she is trying it on, describes the film to an imaginary sales assistant. At first, she is angry with the shallowness of the film but, as she tells its story, is carried away by the escapism it has offered. At their evening meal, to avoid talking to one another or facing up to their difficulties, Sam and Dinah decide to go to the cinema. They will forget their daily problems in the 'bought-and-paid-for magic' of a film called *Trouble in Tahiti*!

Dedicated to Marc Blitzstein, *Trouble in Tahiti* is called 'An Opera in Seven Scenes', but has also been described as an operetta. Musically, it ranges from the 1950s popular song style of the close-harmony group to a melodic *singspiel* which never quite becomes a full-blown aria in the Italian tradition. It is clearly influenced by Blitzstein, who helped with the libretto, and perhaps also by Gian-Carlo Menotti, whose more lyrical *The Medium*, dating from 1946, is sometimes reflected in the sung dialogue. More importantly, it again represented Bernstein's search for an original American music-theatre in its use of naturalistic dialogue in a contemporary musical setting. (Much of the music of *Trouble in Tahiti* is written in 1940s Swing style.) Blitzstein's work had shown him that a libretto did not necessarily call for high-minded prose or poetry; Bernstein's satire is inherited from Brecht and Blitzstein and his choice of mundane language is deliberate. It was a significant development in his career, one which was to return thirty-two years later, when he incorporated it into the framework of his opera *A Quiet Place.*

On 8 September Felicia gave birth to their first child, a daughter named Jamie Anna Maria. Originally, they had chosen the name Nina, after the heroine of an opera on which her godfather Blitzstein was working, but changed it to Jamie out of superstition over an unfinished work. Felicia, who was a star in her own right, returned to television six weeks later and Bernstein made his début in that medium in November, conducting a live telecast of *Trouble in Tahiti.* The irony of the work was apparently lost on most of his critics, who found it dreary in subject, complained of its weak libretto and felt that two emptier, duller people never lived.

Bernstein next turned to a new musical, which developed from one of the most successful dramatic 'vehicles' ever created: a set of autobiographical short stories by Ruth McKenney in *The New Yorker* magazine, based on her youthful adventures as a struggling writer in Greenwich Village in the 1930s. These were adapted into a successful play by Joseph Fields and Jerome Chodorov called *My Sister Eileen*, which then became a film and a radio series. Following that, it was adapted as a stage musical, which in turn became a television musical. It was made into a second (and different) musical film and finally ended up as a highly successful television 'sit-com', running for several seasons. Leonard Bernstein entered the saga in the autumn of 1952, the point at which it was to become a stage musical. The producers Robert Fryer and George Abbott, who had bought the property and signed Rosalind Russell (who had appeared in the first film), invited the team of Comden, Green and Bernstein to write lyrics and music for a new book by Fields and Chodorov. After the success of *On the Town*, this team was the ideal combination for the new show, to be called *Wonderful Town*. In addition, so many of the locations and situations seemed to reflect their own lives and careers.

Fields and Chodorov had adapted their book for the 1950s, but the team persuaded them to go back to the original 1930s setting; this may have caused a few archaic references, but at the same time triggered a wave of enthusiastic nostalgia in Comden, Green and Bernstein. Working round the clock in smoke-filled rooms that would have embarrassed the most case-hardened politicians, they completed the

Following page, Rosalind Russell in a big production scene from Wonderful Town. The assembled cast sing 'The Wrong-note Rag'.

show in five weeks. George Abbott was there to mastermind the production, Bernstein's childhood friend Sid Ramin looked after the orchestrations and Jerome Robbins was brought in (anonymously) to 'doctor' the dance routines for Rosalind Russell who, as a famous Hollywood star, was helping to break box-office records during the try-outs in Boston, Philadelphia and New Haven. *Wonderful Town*, a sparkling, champagne toast to New York, opened at the Winter Garden on 25 February 1953 to unanimously excellent reviews. It was, to all intents and purposes, a musical, but Olin Downes hailed it as 'an opera'. Bernstein, having written some of his finest melodies, was compared with Gershwin (the highest accolade one could achieve on Broadway) and it was described as the best musical since *Guys and Dolls*. Witty not only in its lyrics but in its perfectly integrated score, literate, sophisticated and stylish, it seemed to epitomize the best of the Broadway musical theatre, sweeping the board with Tony Awards, as well as many others, for the 1952–3 season. Sad to say, although they remained lifelong friends and embarked on a number of new projects over the years, it was Bernstein's last collaboration with Comden and Green that bore fruit.

In the late 1940s, America's deep-rooted fear of Communism surfaced through the manipulations of the House Un-American Activities Committee which, in the guise of investigating the operations of genuine subversives, cast a shadow over all creative artists, most of whom had no subversive interests whatsoever, but chose to support liberal causes. The 'kangaroo court' operation of the House Committee severely hampered American creative life for nearly a decade. Many distinguished actors, dancers, authors, playwrights, film directors and others found themselves black-listed because they were smeared with the accusation (and rarely the proof) of supporting Communism or Communist 'front' organizations, or even of being 'fellow-travellers'. More distasteful still were those hearings at which leading figures in the arts and entertainment, eager to save their own skins, named fellow artists.

Even a lighthearted, witty entertainment like *Wonderful Town* came under suspicion, when the television presenter Ed Sullivan, then a columnist for the *Daily News*, 'revealed' that a magazine called the *National Guardian*, supposedly known for its leftist sympathies, had bought a block of tickets for re-sale, and demanded that Rosalind

Russell withdraw from the performance. (The producer, in a panic, cancelled the evening.) In May, Jerome Robbins was called upon to testify before the House Un-American Activities Committee and, to the disgust of many of his friends, identified former colleagues who had been Communists in their idealistically youthful years. Although he only named people who had already been cited, his testimony was regarded as treachery by those who opposed the committee's reign of terror. Another newspaper, the *New York Journal-American*, advised its readers that Bernstein's 'Communist-front record' was well-known to the House Un-American Activities Committee. Fortunately, Bernstein, who had never sought to deny his liberal sympathies, and had openly supported many pro-Russian groups during World War II, was never called upon to testify before the ignoble committee, but he was subjected to the humiliation of a hearing at the State Department (and the services of a very expensive lawyer) when he was initially refused a new passport.

In 1937, when Bernstein first entered Copland's circle of friends, many of New York's musical intelligentsia were liberal if not politically even further left. Bernstein was an impressionable young man and his political thinking was influenced by them. Blitzstein and, later, Jerome Robbins and others also sharpened his social sense but even so, for the most part Bernstein remained remarkably apolitical throughout his life. His major preoccupation was music and many of his critics might have added that this only narrowly superseded his preoccupation with

Senator Joseph McCarthy, whose name became synonymous with America's Communist witch-hunting. This picture was taken during the famous Army hearings, during which the senator's reckless accusations proved to be his downfall.

himself. (Such egotism once caused the pianist Oscar Levant to quip, 'I think a lot about Bernstein – but not as much as he does!') Nevertheless, Bernstein was a loyal Democrat and frequently lent his name to good social causes. In the paranoia that reflected the dark era of McCarthyism, he could easily have been branded a 'Leftie' or fellow-traveller, but he seldom participated actively in genuine left-wing politics. His most deeply felt conviction was an absolute dedication to achieving world peace.

For the summer months, Bernstein was confronted with two festivals: Brandeis, shortly followed by Tanglewood, involving nine or ten weeks of his time and offering little income for his services. His second year at Brandeis chose 'The Comic Spirit' as its theme, with guests like the humorist S. J. Perelman (who, among his many credits, had written the scripts for the Marx Brothers' films), Saul Steinberg and Al Capp, political satirist and creator of the cartoon character 'Li'l Abner'. The music budget had been cut and Bernstein's only concert contribution included a Concerto for Tap Dancer and Orchestra by Morton Gould, and the American première of Francis Poulenc's madcap opera, *Les Mamelles de Tirésias*. It was his last year at Brandeis, from which he resigned. Tanglewood was subdued after the glorious years under Serge Koussevitzky, but Bernstein conducted Mahler's 'Resurrection' Symphony and ran the conducting classes.

In September he returned to Israel (by way of Brazil, on his first visit to South America), where his hectic schedule embraced twenty-one concerts with the Israel Philharmonic in twenty-eight days. He was joined by Felicia and they travelled together to Italy for a series of orchestral concerts. Once again, fate seemed to have a hand in his career, and he proved to be in the right place at the right moment. The distinguished conductor Victor de Sabata, due to appear with Maria Callas in a production of Cherubini's *Medea* at La Scala, was taken ill. Callas had heard Bernstein conduct in a broadcast and suggested that he substitute for de Sabata.

Bernstein had little operatic experience, and did not know Cherubini's work, but he plunged in (at the deep end, as usual), dividing his rehearsals between Milan and a scheduled concert in Rome. He worked with such enthusiasm that the first night was one of the most triumphant and memorable evenings in the history of

The first American conductor to appear at Italy's venerable La Scala opera house in Milan, Bernstein conducted Cherubini's *Medea*, with the legendary Maria Callas.

Italy's greatest opera house. His skill as a conductor drew outstanding playing from the orchestra, and his persuasive powers and instinctive musicianship coaxed Callas into giving one of her greatest and most powerful performances. For many musicians, the world of grand opera is far removed from the concert hall, but Bernstein had seemingly conquered it in his stride. Leonard and Felicia returned home to New York in mid December, but his stay was short as he had to leave for La Scala at the start of 1954 for further performances of *Medea*. Felicia, who was scheduled to appear in three television plays in America, remained in New York. The domestic world of the Bernsteins was forced to play a secondary role in their lives.

Bernstein had originally set aside most of 1954 for work as a composer. He had decided to take a sabbatical from Tanglewood in the summer and would limit himself to a handful of guest appearances at various festivals. In the meantime, offers of composing commissions were mounting up alongside the many attractive invitations to conduct. The violinist Isaac Stern had asked him to write a work for violin and orchestra, and a television company was discussing with Bernstein an opera based on another J. M. Barrie play called *The Boy David*. Perhaps the most attractive project was the proposal by the playwright Lillian Hellman to adapt Voltaire's satirical novel *Candide*, which he had originally rejected. (Andrew Lloyd-Webber fans might be interested to learn that Bernstein and Hellman had also considered but set aside an opera based on the life of Eva Perón.) Just as the machinations of the McCarthy regime prompted Arthur Miller to write *The Crucible* about the Salem witch hunts in the late seventeenth century, the work of Voltaire, who had espoused a call for tolerance and free thought in the eighteenth century, appealed to Bernstein and to Hellman, who had also suffered the ugly insinuations of the House Committee.

Before he could begin work on what was going to be almost a lifetime of writing and rewriting Voltaire's masterpiece, Bernstein was sidetracked into composing the music for Elia Kazan's classic film *On the Waterfront*, with screenplay by Budd Schulberg and starring Marlon Brando, Eva Marie Saint, Rod Steiger, Lee J. Cobb and Karl Malden. At first he had been unwilling to collaborate with Kazan, who had been one of the Un-American Activities Committee's informers. It was the producer Sam Spiegel who persuaded Bernstein to view a rough cut of the film; the composer was so moved by it that he agreed to provide the score. (The assignment had the added advantage of carrying a substantial fee, which would make up for some of the lost income from the concert appearances that he had turned down during this year of writing.)

Despite his contacts, however, Bernstein had earlier hesitated before committing himself to film projects; and writing for the screen proved to be an exacting discipline, allowing him little of the leeway to which, as a composer, he was normally accustomed. He had always admired the film scores of Aaron Copland, who had first worked in Hollywood in the late 1930s and whose credits included Thornton

Marlon Brando in Elia Kazan's film *On the Waterfront,* for which Bernstein composed a remarkable score

Wilder's classic *Our Town* and John Steinbeck's *Of Mice and Men.* Copland had written, in *Our New Music,* that a film score was designed to intensify the emotional impact of the drama and create an illusion of continuity, but Bernstein realized all too soon that his score would always be an accompaniment to the visual drama. Sometimes, it was faded below or drowned out by the dialogue; at others, it had to share a soundtrack with the natural sounds of the waterfront, from cranes to ships' sirens. Worse still, an entire sequence could find itself accompanying an altered scene to the cutting-room floor. In an article in the *New York Times,* he described himself pleading for 'a beloved G flat', adding that the only comfort he received was the suggestion that he could always use the lost parts in a suite.

Despite the difficulties, Bernstein mastered the technique with consummate skill, creating one of the most memorable film scores of the 1950s. Just as Bernard Herrmann's music became an integral part of a Hitchcock thriller (we remember the screaming strings as much as the visual images of the murder in *Psycho*), the music of *On the Waterfront* added immeasurably to the dramatic power of the story. But although the film won eight Academy Awards, it was the veteran Dimitri Tiomkin who was awarded the Oscar for Best Musical Score with *The High and the Mighty*, a John Wayne epic, and one of the first airline 'disaster movies'.

Bernstein never composed another film score, although he was invited to do so on a number of occasions. It could be that he found the technique too confining, or simply that his free time for composition was too precious to him. Fortunately, he remembered the advice he had received in Hollywood and later created a Symphonic Suite from the film in 1955. Played without a break, it makes use of the various original themes and also salvages some of the material that was '... left on the floor of the dubbing-room'. While it makes a lasting souvenir of Elia Kazan's film, it is also a powerful and free-standing orchestral work in its own right which, rather like *The Age of Anxiety*, can survive independently of the creation that inspired it.

Bernstein seemed to go through peaks and troughs of creativity. There would be periods of inactivity, during which he restricted himself to conducting, but once the juices started to flow, and provided there were not too many distractions, he worked quickly and with intense concentration. It may have been this ability that caused Aaron Copland, despite their friendship, to use the unflattering word 'facile' when assessing his ability as a composer.

In the summer of 1954 the family rented a house on the island of Martha's Vineyard off the Massachusetts coast where, with 'all cylinders firing', Bernstein settled down to work on two projects: the violin concerto for Isaac Stern, which he finished quite rapidly, and *Candide*, which progressed very slowly. By early September, when he had to leave for the première of the violin work with Stern and the Israel Philharmonic in Venice, only the first half of *Candide* was in any sort of shape.

Bernstein's 'violin concerto', commissioned by the Koussevitzky Foundation and dedicated to the memory of Serge and Natalie

Koussevitzky, is his *Serenade, after Plato's 'Symposium'*, for solo violin, string orchestra, harp and percussion. He chose the title *Serenade* after the Italian *sera*, or 'evening' piece, and the reference to the *Symposium* (Plato's examination of the many aspects of love as defined by his Athenian colleagues) is, like Auden's *The Age of Anxiety* or, for that matter, Kazan's *On the Waterfront*, simply the *idea* that triggered the music. If anything, the title is misleading and Bernstein's references to Aristophanes, Erixymachus, Socrates, Alcibiades and the others serve only as a guide to the sequences in the *Symposium* (which he had read at Harvard and re-read on one of his trips to Cuernavaca) that inspired his musical ideas. His work is, in essence, in praise of love in every sense of the word, a theme which was a guiding principle of his life, and his *Serenade* strives to express, through music, his love for humankind.

It is one of Leonard Bernstein's finest works and, like others, needs no programmatic explanations. Of more interest are the musical 'evolutionary' techniques that Bernstein employs in the work, in which the melodies in each of the five movements (played almost without pause) evolve from thematic material in the preceding movement and, at times, even within the context of the same movement. Perhaps the most important fact, however, is that one can listen to the entire thirty-minute *Serenade* without any foreknowledge of its 'programme' or technical skills and enjoy it simply as a very accessible, partly jazz-influenced work of fine art that belongs to the middle years of this century.

At the time, the reviews were, as usual, mixed. Italian musical cognoscenti were still in the dour grip of serialism and highly suspicious of anything that contained elements of jazz. Virgil Thomson, reporting for the *Herald-Tribune*, was always ready to put in a bad word. It fared better at its première in New York the following year, although Howard Taubman in the *Times* still worried whether jazz in any form belonged in the concert hall. Future conductors and violinists may have the musical wisdom to ensure that it becomes a permanent work in the repertory.

In the autumn Bernstein returned to New York with *Candide* firmly in his sights, but was again sidetracked by a fascinating project which was to lead him into a new chapter of his musical life. In those far-off days when American television networks supported arts projects, CBS featured a magazine programme, funded by the Ford Foundation, called 'Omnibus'. The producers invited him to present a programme about Beethoven's Fifth Symphony – a work whose first movement virtually everybody would recognize. Working with Beethoven's notebooks, Bernstein would illustrate, by playing some of the material the composer had rejected and restoring it into the body of the work, the many changes wrought by Beethoven during the creation of his great 'battlefield' of a masterpiece.

Bernstein prepared a brilliant script. Standing on an enlarged reproduction of the opening page of Beethoven's symphony, he pointed out the opening notes that signal the famous 'dot-dot-dot-dash' of the music. Musicians holding appropriate instruments stood on the orchestral staves of the score, so that the viewer was presented with a human representation of the orchestral forces that make the sounds of the symphony. By conducting the sections that Beethoven did not eventually use and offering probable reasons for their

The first 'Omnibus' programme on television, 14 November 1954, during which Bernstein discussed and illustrated the creation of Beethoven's Fifth Symphony

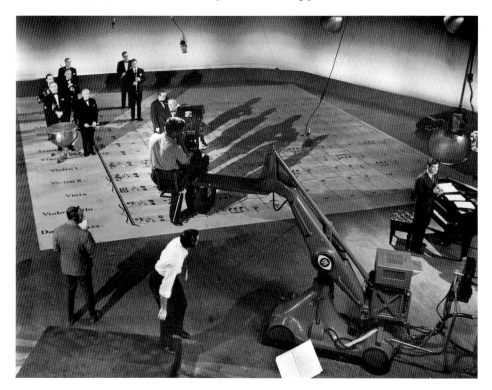

rejection, Bernstein showed the absolute logic of the composer's final choices. He spoke for about twenty minutes, displaying all the skill and persuasiveness of a great actor and, to end the programme, conducted the complete first movement of the symphony as it is known today.

It was a thrilling, compelling programme, bringing about an immediate national response, and it marked the start of a television career that would take him through more than fifty programmes, establishing a new and dedicated audience. (As a matter of interest, the programme was broadcast live on one of Bernstein's 'key' dates: 14 November 1954, eleven years to the day after his unexpected New York Philharmonic début, and seventeen years to the day after his first chance meeting with Aaron Copland.)

The 'Omnibus' programme was a triumph, but it meant that, once again, *Candide* fell by the wayside. John Latouche had originally been brought in to write the lyrics (to Lillian Hellman's ponderous book) but parted company with Hellman and Bernstein in November. Bernstein and Felicia had written the lyrics to one song ('I Am Easily Assimilated') the previous summer and it was suggested for a while that Bernstein should take on all the lyrics (which he might have succeeded in doing had he not had so many other commitments).

For the moment, the project had to be shelved while Bernstein was in Italy for further appearances at La Scala with Maria Callas. There was a new production of *La sonnambula* by Bellini directed by Luchino Visconti, as well as a revival of *La bohème*. Although he was joined by Felicia (expecting their second child) for some of the time, Bernstein was in Italy for four months. In his absence, Isaac Stern gave the American première of the *Serenade* in Boston with Charles Munch, and *Trouble in Tahiti*, accompanied on two pianos, was presented on Broadway with great success as part of a triple bill of one-act plays.

While staying in Rome with Visconti, Bernstein was attracted to the idea of developing a musical based on the novel *Serenade* by James M. Cain (who also wrote *The Postman Always Rings Twice*). When he returned to New York, despite his good intentions towards *Candide*, he was faced with a project bogged down in endless problems: no satisfactory lyrics and unresolved discussions with the producer over who should direct or star in the show, *if* it ever saw completion. His thoughts were still on Cain's *Serenade* and he discussed it with the playwright Arthur Laurents (whose moving play *Home of the Brave*, about anti-Semitism, had later been transmogrified into a film about racial discrimination). At that moment, Jerome Robbins intervened to plead again the cause of a musical idea he had suggested as far back as January of 1949: a modern adaptation of *Romeo and Juliet*, set in urban America, in which feelings run high between Catholic Capulets and Jewish Montagues. The working title was *East Side Story*. Even then, because of *Home of the Brave*, Laurents had been the Robbins/Bernstein choice to write the book. Once more filled with enthusiasm, Bernstein shelved *Serenade* and, for the moment, the troublesome *Candide*.

In early July, the Bernsteins' second child, Alexander Serge (named in honour of Koussevitzky), was born. Bernstein had just completed the symphonic suite from *On the Waterfront*, which he dedicated to his new son, and the work received its première the following month at Tanglewood. From there, he travelled to Los Angeles to take part in a short-lived Festival of the Americas. While he was there, a newspaper item about gang warfare between Mexican immigrants and young Los Angeleans caught Bernstein's attention. He discussed the idea with Arthur Laurents and, musically stimulated by the prospect of incorporating Latin-American dance rhythms into the framework of the story, they agreed to move *East Side Story* to New York, with its Puerto Rican community.

By the end of August, Bernstein was demonstrating the extraordinary diversity of his creative powers, dividing his attention between the new project and the ever-present *Candide*. He had also agreed to compose incidental music for yet another theatrical venture: Lillian Hellman's translation of Jean Anouilh's play *L'Alouette* ('The Lark') about Joan of Arc. Following her battles with McCarthy, Hellman no doubt identified with Saint Joan's suffering at the hands of her English tribunal. As if all these projects were not enough, Bernstein was in addition preparing his second 'Omnibus' television programme called 'The World of Jazz'; it was to be an illustrated history of the medium, which gave Bernstein the opportunity to present his *Prelude, Fugue and Riffs*, the piece that he had written as a commission for Woody Herman three years earlier, and which the bandleader had never played (nor paid for!).

Prelude, Fugue and Riffs is scored for solo clarinet, five saxophones, four trumpets, four trombones, piano, percussion and string bass – a typical 'Big Band' line-up – and although purists could argue that it is not strictly jazz, because the players do not improvise most of the music, it should be pointed out that by the late 1940s and early 50s jazz had taken many – often sophisticated – forms, from the quasi-symphonic orchestrations of the Duke Ellington orchestra to the Big Band music of Stan Kenton or the stylish arrangements of Gil Evans. Bernstein's piece could be categorized as 1950s Big Band, but also harks back to the 1940s Swing era of Artie Shaw or Benny Goodman, who made the first recording and to whom the work was eventually dedicated.

The Prelude is played by the brass, followed by a Fugue for saxophones. The Riffs – a popular jazz and swing device in which short rhythmic/melodic phrases are repeated over changing harmonies – are introduced by the solo clarinet and piano, after which the whole band joins in to create an effective 'jam session'. It is an exhilarating piece and a performance on record by the clarinettist Peter Schmidl with members of no less an ensemble than the Vienna Philharmonic Orchestra, directed by Bernstein, shows that such music need not necessarily be the exclusive property of American jazz musicians.

In the autumn, Lillian Hellman's play *The Lark*, starring Julie Harris, opened to an excellent reception and ran for almost a year. Bernstein received special mention for his *a cappella* score suggesting the voices that inspired Joan of Arc. He never discarded good material, simply shelving it for later suitable occasions, and would eventually use this music, written in an antique style, in his *Missa brevis*.

Throughout most of this period, Bernstein had set aside conducting assignments in America. He had appeared at Tanglewood and, briefly, at the Los Angeles festival, but still had no orchestra of his own. For the first of his 'Omnibus' programmes, he had used the Symphony of the Air, formerly known as the NBC Symphony, and familiarly known as 'The Toscanini Orchestra', because the broadcasting company had created it in the late 1930s for the great Italian maestro. Toscanini retired in 1954 aged eighty-seven, and although NBC had no desire to maintain the organization, the players were struggling to stay together, calling themselves 'the orchestra that refused to die'. They had even managed a far-eastern tour in the spring of the year and were planning a further tour in 1956.

In November 1955 Bernstein conducted the first of six Carnegie Hall concerts with the Symphony of the Air. Olin Downes, who had always championed Bernstein's work in the *New York Times*, had died the preceding August but his successor Howard Taubman was equally supportive. It was a temporary situation, providing Bernstein with useful income and keeping him before concert audiences. Behind the scenes, Bruno Zirato was organizing stronger ties with the New York Philharmonic. Rodzinski had left in 1947, after losing a power struggle with Arthur Judson and from 1949 the orchestra had been led by Bernstein's old friend, Dimitri Mitropoulos. By the following November Bernstein would be made joint Principal Conductor with Mitropoulos, starting in the autumn of 1957. His association with the Symphony of the Air might have lasted longer had not the old anti-Communist bogey reared its head, almost for the last time in Bernstein's case. (There was the suggestion that the FBI infiltrated the orchestra of *Candide*, in view of its anti-government 'attitude', but it was never proved.)

In March of the following year, a Washington sub-committee alleged that some of the orchestra's members were Communist 'fellow-travellers'. When he was younger, Bernstein was always adding his name to committees and good causes; first, because he espoused liberal ideals, but more often for the self-confessed reason that a little extra publicity never did any harm. Some of the time, it is unlikely that he even knew what purpose many of these committees served, as long as, in the words of the old saw, they 'spelled his name right'.

Bernstein was never identified by the sub-committee, but it was clear that he was the target. The orchestra's 1956 tour was cancelled, but Bernstein was not questioned further. One possible reason for this was that his fourth 'Omnibus' programme (the third had been a brilliant commentary on the art of conducting) was about Harvard University, and he shared it with Senator John F. Kennedy, who became a good friend. It is probable that Kennedy was able to reassure his Washington associates that Bernstein did not represent any threat to American national security.

In the meantime, his two theatre projects were progressing. Comden and Green had been approached for *East Side Story*, but had turned it down, and Bernstein finally decided to co-author the lyrics with Stephen Sondheim, a family friend of Oscar Hammerstein II who had been a music major and had trained as a composer. Sondheim's musical background, together with a mutual fascination with words and anagrams, made him an ideal partner for Bernstein. During the gestation period of the project they discovered that many of the upper east-side Manhattan tenements had been pulled down to make way for new housing projects, driving most of the residents across the city; the name of the new show was therefore changed to *West Side Story*. They had completed much of it by January of 1956.

Bernstein could now turn his attention to *Candide*. During the winter, Richard Wilbur (a young poet who had recently made a superb translation of Molière's *Le Misanthrope*), had been recruited to write the lyrics. He set to work, producing new songs and polishing the existing material, while Bernstein amused himself with some guest appearances as a panellist on television, where he was already becoming a familiar figure. By May, the family was again installed on Martha's Vineyard and was joined by Wilbur and the distinguished director Tyrone Guthrie, who had been brought in to direct. Despite occasional absences – concerts at Lewisohn Stadium and a festival of his own works in Chicago – Bernstein's attention was focused on *Candide*.

The first version (and there would be at least six more attempts during Bernstein's lifetime to make it work) was completed in the summer months of 1956. While there is little question that it contains some of his finest and wittiest music, it was forever hampered by its book and some of its lyrics. Perhaps, from the start, its authors and many contributing lyricists (who included, by 1989, John Latouche, Dorothy Parker, Lillian Hellman, Leonard and Felicia Bernstein, Stephen Sondheim and John Wells) could never quite agree on what it set out to achieve. Lillian Hellman had originally conceived a play with music, not unlike *The Lark*. As a serious playwright, she had not planned (and was ill-equipped to write) a musical comedy. In addition, her underlying motive had been to attack political intolerance in contemporary America. On the other hand, Bernstein's contribution, which he described as 'comic operetta', was in turn satirical ('Glitter and Be Gay' is a brilliant and endearing pastiche of every *coloratura* aria ever composed), cynical ('Am Easily Assimiliated' speaks for itself), sentimental ('Oh Happy We' is one of the most beautiful melodies he ever wrote), mocking ('The Best of All Possible Worlds' has echoes of W. S. Gilbert), and touchingly optimistic

('Make Our Garden Grow' may not reflect Voltaire's cruel wit, but it underlines his message of hope). The Overture is a standard concert hall item and is performed regularly the world over.

It could be that Voltaire's novella, with its constant changes of location and a satirical wit that is best appreciated on the printed page, will never ideally translate to the stage. (It might, one day, be adapted yet again to the wider possibilities of the screen.) The show opened in Boston in the autumn of 1956, starring Robert Rounseville (who had appeared in the pioneering film of Offenbach's *The Tales of Hoffman*, conducted by Sir Thomas Beecham, as well as the world première of Stravinsky's *The Rake's Progress*). Max Adrian (a sophisticated revue artist from London) was Dr Pangloss, and Barbara Cook (who had had small roles in *Oklahoma!* and *Carousel*) played Cunegonde. That none of them was well-known to Broadway theatregoers did not help the advance sales for a very expensive production. The sets were by Oliver Smith, the lavish costumes by Irene Sharaff (two Bernstein 'faithfuls') and the orchestrations, except for the Overture, by Hershy Kay.

The reviews were very uneasy, using dangerous words like 'esoteric' and 'satire' that could easily discourage audiences. Following drastic cuts, rewrites and changes, it opened at the Martin Beck Theatre in New York on 1 December 1956. Once again, it was given a very mixed reception. Interestingly, the majority of the critics were positive – a few were hostile – but the real problem was that *Candide* was not a traditional Broadway musical: no romantic plot, no memorable tunes that would be picked up by 'cover' records featuring popular singers of the day and played by the disc-jockeys. It was too close to an opera and, for many typical musical-comedy fans, too clever for its own good. The run closed after seventy-three performances and showing a financial loss. It was Bernstein's first Broadway 'flop'.

In spite of its failure, a number of people recognized Bernstein's creative achievement. Goddard Lieberson of Columbia Records made a memorable Original Cast recording, in which the qualities of the songs and the performers are self-evident. (As a matter of interest, Tom Shepard, himself a distinguished producer of show albums, later discovered that the CBS engineers, experimenting with new techniques, had made a trial stereophonic recording – some years before stereo was introduced – which had been resting, unreleased, in the tape vaults. It was issued in the 1960s.)

Robert Rounseville
(Candide) and Barbara Cook
(Cunegonde) in the original
1956 production of *Candide*

It took many years and rewrites for *Candide* finally to find its rightful place as an operetta, including versions dating from 1957, 1959, 1966, 1967, 1968 and 1971. Harold Prince (one of the producers of *West Side Story*) revived it in 1973 as a reworked one-act entertainment at the Chelsea Theatre in Brooklyn. Stephen Sondheim provided some extra lyrics, and a new book by Hugh Wheeler greatly reduced Lillian Hellman's efforts at satire or political commentary, emphasizing instead the farcical humour. The production was then expanded and transferred successfully to Broadway for a run of nearly two years, but Bernstein was still unhappy with it. Voltaire's satirical wit had been watered down, much of his favourite writing had been taken out and the cast was accompanied by a minimal orchestra, conducted by John Mauceri, that relied too much on electronic keyboards. In addition, the music had been reshuffled and was now sung by different characters. In 1982, a further enlarged two-act Prince-and-Wheeler 'opera house' version was presented by the New York City Opera, again directed by Prince and conducted by Mauceri; it came closer to the full operetta, but still presented much of the score out of its original context. It was, however, well received, especially by the serious music critics. Six years later, John Mauceri, now at the Scottish Opera and this time working with Bernstein, devised a version that was musically true to the original. Jonathan Miller, assisted by the writer John Wells, who added further lyrics, directed the new production. The additional changes received Bernstein's full blessing and the production was later presented by the Old Vic in London in 1989. Bernstein eventually recorded the final revision later in the same year. It would therefore take thirty-three years for him to achieve a version with which he was satisfied.

Meanwhile, in December 1956, Bernstein renewed his association with the New York Philharmonic. The announcement that he would be installed as joint conductor with Mitropoulos from the following season had already been made, but his first appearance with the orchestra, after an absence of some years, took place earlier than anticipated, due to the tragic death of Guido Cantelli in an air crash in Paris. He conducted Cantelli's programmes, following them with his own (including a controversial *Messiah* that was lambasted by Paul Henry Lang of the *Herald-Tribune*, who, after inheriting the job from Virgil Thomson, continued the attack on Bernstein).

It was becoming clear, however, that Bernstein was more than likely to take over the reins of the New York Philharmonic, and his career was moving rapidly forward again. He was on the cover of *Time* magazine, the first occasion on which an American conductor had been so honoured and his extended appearances with the orchestra had enjoyed substantial public acclaim. Having renewed his Columbia Records contract, he recorded a number of works, including concertos with Isaac Stern and Glenn Gould, and also found time to prepare his next 'Omnibus' programme, dealing with contemporary music. The programme, entitled 'An Introduction to Modern Music', took on the monumental task of explaining to a mass television audience that the complex music of the twentieth century was no less 'beautiful' than the seemingly simpler music of the past. For the musicians in his audience Bernstein made it clear that his preference in contemporary music lay with Copland and Stravinsky (of that era) rather than with Arnold Schoenberg and his followers in the so-called Second Viennese School. (In the following programme, discussing the music of J. S. Bach and performing excerpts from the *St Matthew Passion* and the *Magnificat*, Bernstein displayed not only his enthusiasm but also a deep knowledge and understanding of a composer whose music he had rarely performed at any time in his career.)

By the spring of 1957, he had also agreed to take on the 'Young People's Concerts' with the New York Philharmonic, four of which would later be televised each year by CBS. As far as the general public was concerned, *Candide* was forgotten and Leonard Bernstein was all

Bernstein surrounded by youthful admirers at one of his 'Young People's Concerts'

set to resume his former career, triumphantly returning to the concert platform as the permanent head of one of America's most distinguished orchestras. But within four months, his name would again light up the Broadway sky, this time with a success that would shape the rest of his life. Following try-outs in Washington and Philadelphia, *West Side Story* opened in New York at the Winter Garden Theatre on 26 September 1957.

3

An early caricature of
Bernstein by Don Bevan –
one of the trappings of
stardom

*His role was as the gentle teacher, the logical,
compassionate, caring and articulate teacher,
who inspired you so that you wanted to please
him more than life itself.*

Carol Lawrence, the original Maria in *West
Side Story* (in *Conversations about Bernstein*)

Years of Glory 1957–69

Back in 1938, one of the qualities that had attracted Bernstein to *The Cradle Will Rock* was the manner in which Blitzstein had adapted colloquial language, in melody and in rhythm, to create a specifically American music-theatre that could replace the familiar melodies and couplets of the traditional Broadway musical – much as Bernstein loved them and had grown up with them – with something more effectively meaningful.

Throughout his 'Broadway' years, which reached their apex in *West Side Story*, Bernstein sought to bring an original voice to the musical theatre. He would never have achieved this fully with Comden and Green. Witty, sophisticated and urbane, they wrote in the tradition of Cole Porter, and were, so to speak, the next generation on. While Bernstein's scores for *On the Town* and *Wonderful Town* certainly added a distinctive, original style to their words, Comden and Green were even better suited to an old-fashioned 'tunesmith' like Jule Styne, who gave them the ideal score with *Bells Are Ringing*. As a composer, Bernstein was still moving forward with each new project. History has shown that *Candide* never belonged on Broadway in the first place and would take more than thirty years to find its home in the opera house.

What probably made *West Side Story* unique was that it was a Broadway musical (Bernstein called it a 'tragic musical comedy') created, in Jerome Robbins's words, by 'long-hair' artists (at this time a hirsute appearance was still the province of a classical artist). Arthur Laurents was a serious playwright. In addition to *Home of the Brave*, he had written the bitter-sweet *The Time of the Cuckoo*, which he rewrote for the screen as *Summertime*, with Katherine Hepburn and Rossano Brazzi, as well as *A Clearing in the Woods*, a new play for Broadway. Other screen credits included *Anastasia* and *The Snake Pit*. Stephen Sondheim had studied under Milton Babbitt at Princeton, but he loved the theatre and, like Bernstein, enjoyed playing with words. When Bernstein had originally offered him the job of co-

An encounter of the star-crossed lovers in the original stage production of *West Side Story*, September 1957

authoring the lyrics, he was not very interested, but accepted the role on the advice of Hammerstein, who suggested it would be useful experience. Robbins, too, had moved away from his true calling as a classically trained dancer and choreographer to work on musical shows. Even the designer Oliver Smith, whose moody sets created the perfect New York backdrop, had originally started out as a serious painter. It was the combination of all these talents, with fresh ideas, a new approach, and fewer hardboiled convictions as to what made a Broadway show 'work' (from a traditional chorus line to a standard comedy character), that turned *West Side Story* into both a work of art and a pioneering example of contemporary music-theatre, without the pretensions that such titles often suggest.

The creation of the show progressed reasonably smoothly. In the end, Sondheim wrote all the lyrics, polishing those on which Bernstein had started work and adding those that he had completed alone. (In a typically generous gesture, and in a manner rare in the cut-throat annals of Broadway, Bernstein insisted that Sondheim receive full credit for his work, and the posters for the show as well as the printed scores were changed to reflect this.) There was a moment of drama when, shortly before the production was due to begin rehearsals, the producer Cheryl Crawford decided to withdraw. Sondheim came to the rescue, bringing in his friend Harold Prince who, with his partner Robert Griffith, had already produced three

Following page, Bernstein rehearsing the cast of *West Side Story*. Carol Lawrence (Maria) is on Bernstein's left, and the lyricist Stephen Sondheim is seated at the piano.

Broadway hits: *The Pajama Game*, *Damn Yankees* and *New Girl in Town*. Within a week, they raised the necessary $300,000. There was a lot at risk, especially as the cast consisted of virtual 'unknowns'.

Throughout the preparation of the show, Bernstein was at his most co-operative, possibly because *Candide* had taught him that he did not have an infallible touch, but most probably because he trusted his collaborators – particularly Jerome Robbins – implicitly. All the participants received and exchanged ideas with mutual respect. Two different opening choruses were eventually dropped in favour of the dazzling finger-snapping ballet that sets the show in motion. Both 'Somewhere' (whose melody originally took shape during *On the Town*) and 'One Hand, One Heart' were originally intended for the fire-escape/balcony scene, but were moved to later episodes at the suggestion of Laurents and Robbins; Bernstein and Sondheim replaced the songs with the quasi-operatic 'Tonight', one of the great show-stoppers of the production. Originally there was only dialogue to introduce the hero Tony, but some of Arthur Laurents's words were 'borrowed' to create the song 'Something's Coming', letting music underscore the anticipatory mood of the moment.

As Bernstein was working on the scores of both *Candide* and *West Side Story* over much of the same period, a surprising amount of cross-fertilization took place. 'One Hand, One Heart' and the music for 'Gee, Officer Krupke' were originally written for *Candide*, while 'O Happy We', seemingly irrevocably linked to *Candide*, was actually written for a scene discarded from *West Side Story*. This seems to indicate clearly enough that Bernstein, when not composing for the concert hall or the opera house, was writing for 'music-theatre', whether it was a satire by Voltaire or a *Romeo and Juliet* set in the tenements of Manhattan.

Following strenuous New York rehearsals (the cast are dancers as much as singers or actors), the show was to move to Washington for a three-week trial run, to be followed by a two-week stay in Philadelphia. Jerome Robbins, who was director and, with the assistance of Peter Gennaro, choreographer (in addition, a line stated that the show was based on his conception), put everyone, including Bernstein, through their paces. Applying the 'Method' school of acting, Robbins made the opposing gangs of Jets and Sharks live their parts, wearing suitably emblazoned jackets, and encouraged antagonism between them, offstage as well as on. There is also a frequently repeated story concerning his changing the score at the Washington dress rehearsal, deleting notes without permission, which Bernstein meekly accepted, swallowing his pride alongside several glasses of scotch.

In his biography, Humphrey Burton includes extracts from a touching exchange of letters between Bernstein and Felicia, who had taken the children to Chile for a holiday (and, presumably, to leave him undisturbed during the critical period of final preparation). His love for and dependence upon her are apparent in every line, just as her strength and support are always there to sustain him, urging him to fight against 'all that mediocrity' for what he believes in. Tired and nervous, he is struggling to retain those parts of his score that he loves best, only to be told that they are too 'operatic'. Swearing that it is the last show he will do, he fears that everything will be sacrificed on the altar of commercial success, which he believes can be still be achieved, but 'with pride'. The loving intimacy of their correspondence is very moving. (In the midst of this, he was also able to report with glee that he had signed his new contract with the New York Philharmonic, tearing up the twenty-page legal document and replacing it with a one-page letter of engagement.)

The opening night in Washington was greeted with 'rave' reviews in the press. Bernstein was fêted wherever he went, and this included a lunch at the White House. (It was during the Washington run that he credited all the lyrics to Stephen Sondheim.) Philadelphia enjoyed equal success, but press reaction to the New York première, while excellent, was a little more reserved. Jerome Robbins was praised unanimously for his choreography, but one reviewer questioned his skill as a director. Brooks Atkinson was totally positive, but Howard Taubman wondered whether Bernstein had not capitulated too much to Broadway. Walter Kerr in the *Herald-Tribune* criticized the singing. *West Side Story*, nevertheless, repaid its producers handsomely. The initial Broadway run was 732 performances, followed by a national tour that lasted nearly a year. In 1960, it reopened in New York for a further 253 performances. The original cast recording on Columbia Records sold over one million copies. The Tony award for Best Musical in 1957, however, went to Meredith Willson's 'old-fashioned' show *The Music Man*, starring Robert Preston.

Jerome Robbins demonstrates
a move prior to filming a
scene of *West Side Story*.

The real rewards would come from the film of *West Side Story*. At
the time of its sale to Hollywood, it was not considered a particularly
valuable property, and Harold Prince and his investors were given a
substantial share of the gross income. It proved to be a phenomenal,
worldwide success, winning the Oscar for Best Picture of 1961,
together with nine other Academy Awards. Although Bernstein had
little personally to do with the production (and did not qualify for an
award because his score was not an original work written for the
screen), the film probably did more to establish his name
internationally than anything else he ever did.

The success of *West Side Story*, preceded by a *Candide* which had
been treated respectfully by the press despite its financial loss, made
Bernstein one of the 'hottest' potential properties on Broadway by the
autumn of 1957, yet it was at that moment that he turned away from
the musical theatre for more than a decade (and, in the next twelve
years or more, composed only two major symphonic works). The

distinguished theatre critic, Brooks Atkinson, who spent thirty-five years at the *New York Times*, noted in his book *Broadway* that Bernstein 'capitulated to respectability'.

Whether or not 'respectability' was Bernstein's motive in accepting the appointment with the New York Philharmonic (the reason he offered was that it would simplify his life and give him more time to think about music), his appointment came as a shock to musical circles. He was originally appointed joint conductor of the orchestra with Mitropoulos, to start in January 1958, but on his return in November 1957 from a visit to Israel, where he had inaugurated the new Frederic R. Mann Hall in Tel Aviv (and during which he began conducting with a baton), the orchestra called a press conference to announce that, from September 1958, Bernstein would be its first American-born Music Director (his predecessors had been called *Musical* Directors). In addition to conducting, he was to plan the season's format, determine the content of programmes, select and co-ordinate guest conductors and soloists, handle the orchestra's personnel problems, study scores and plan concert tours, including choosing programmes and assisting artists. Apart from score studying, all these responsibilities had previously been the domain of the orchestra's manager. It was therefore a position of major importance in the music world, at the head of one of America's most powerful and influential organizations, and it came about because, in addition to having the talent for the task, Leonard Bernstein was once again in the right place at the right time.

The reasons for the New York Philharmonic to make such structural changes can be attributed to a newspaper article, written in the *New York Times* in April 1956 by its chief critic, Howard Taubman. For some time, the state of the Philharmonic and the way it was run had been a matter of concern to those who cared about the orchestral life of the city. Subscription figures and general ticket sales had been falling, programmes had become run-of-the-mill, visiting soloists were of indifferent quality, and the public seemed to have lost interest. Taubman's testimony, a musical equivalent of Émil Zola's *J'accuse*, took the form of an extended essay entitled 'The Philharmonic – What's Wrong with It and Why'; it occupied the entire music page of the Sunday edition. Taubman analysed the orchestra's difficulties, highlighting specific problems. His first target was Dimitri

Mitropoulos who, while he could still thrill audiences, revealed too many important gaps in his repertoire. His most frequent guest conductors, Walter and Szell, preferred conservative programmes and, although Mitropoulos had increased the Philharmonic's range, many important twentieth-century works by major composers had never been heard. In addition, he was too easy-going, permitting serious lapses of discipline in an orchestra that had traditionally displayed an independent attitude. Furthermore, Mitropoulos appeared to have little planning in his programming or his choice of guest artists. As Taubman saw it, the orchestra was demoralized and was becoming a second-class musical organization.

His article then moved to the real cause of the problems faced by the orchestra, one that had been apparent to anyone working in the American music world for the past quarter of a century. Arthur Judson, head of the all-powerful Columbia Artists Management Inc. (CAMI), supplying most of the musicians appearing in concerts anywhere in the United States, was also firmly ensconced as the Manager of the New York Philharmonic. Taubman concluded that

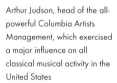

Arthur Judson, head of the all-powerful Columbia Artists Management, which exercised a major influence on all classical musical activity in the United States

the conflict of interests should no longer be tolerated by the Philharmonic's board, and suggested that the orchestra should have an independent management, similar to the orchestras of Boston, Philadelphia and other cities.

Taubman's observations were regarded as something of a bombshell, even though he was only voicing sentiments that had been felt for a long time. During his years with the Philharmonic, Artur Rodzinski had crossed swords regularly with Judson, and lost on numerous occasions. When offered a new contract, Rodzinski had again challenged the manager's absolute dictatorship, insisting that he should have more say in the planning of the season's programmes, including his own and those of guest conductors. Judson, whose musical tastes were conservative and strongly influenced by box-office receipts, controlled the choice of programmes and soloists, often basing his decisions on the fees his CAMI artists would receive. (In this area, Taubman surely attacked the wrong man when he blamed Mitropoulos.) When Rodzinski had directed the orchestras in Cleveland and Los Angeles, he attended board meetings, but Judson excluded him in New York, appointing himself as spokesman. The fiery conductor, whose quick temper may well have weakened his cause, challenged Judson on every count, but the board backed its manager and Rodzinski resigned, to be replaced by Mitropoulos.

Perhaps the Board of the Philharmonic had naïvely believed that their dignified and courteous manager was too much of a gentleman to stoop to such behaviour but, for years, Judson as manager of the orchestra, had been hiring – at preferential fees – artists represented by Judson of CAMI. (Today, the world's larger managements still use their power and influence to bring pressure to bear on orchestras and other musical associations, albeit not quite as crudely. Certain *quid pro quo* agreements often find their way into the negotiations surrounding the hiring of a lesser-known soloist or even the appointment of a new conductor.)

Arthur Judson's retirement from the orchestra was announced a discreet six months after Taubman's article. Had he remained, he would probably have vetoed Bernstein's appointment, despite their initial relationship (which had always been looked after by Bruno Zirato). Many years earlier, Judson had mapped out a plan by which Bernstein could have become the Philharmonic's musical director by the age of thirty, but Bernstein had turned him down, insisting that he needed freedom to compose.

Taubman's essay had ended with a number of constructive suggestions. There should be a new musical director in place of Mitropoulos; cogent programmes should be developed and appropriate guest artists chosen to perform them. In addition, to restore its position at the forefront of American music, the Philharmonic should be brought before the largest possible audience. The article was strongly supported by Taubman's colleagues in the musical press, who added commentaries of their own.

Shortly after Judson's 'retirement', Mitropoulos, who had earlier suffered a heart attack and whose health was clearly failing, accepted what appeared to be a compromise at the Philharmonic, with the announcement that he had requested the orchestra to engage Leonard Bernstein to share the direction of the orchestra, starting with the 1957–8 season. The reasons he gave were that he had received a large number of invitations to appear with European orchestras and that he wanted to increase his activities with the Metropolitan Opera. How seriously he had asked for Bernstein is not clear. Despite their friendship, Mitropoulos had spent little time with his protégé of earlier years and since taking over in 1950 had not invited him to be a guest conductor of the orchestra at Carnegie Hall. But ever since his New York City Symphony days, and whenever he appeared, Bernstein had shown himself to be an innovative and imaginative programmer, an excellent partner to complement the work of Mitropoulos.

The New York Philharmonic had obviously been moved to action by Taubman's article. Its President, David M. Keiser, referred to 'valuable recommendations'. Judson was out of the way, and a halfway-house arrangement had been reached by coupling Bernstein with Mitropoulos. They were also mindful of Taubman's exhortation to bring the orchestra to the attention of the largest possible audience. No medium could achieve this better than television, bringing the symphony orchestra into the living-rooms of millions of viewers, and no conductor was more articulate or skilled in doing it than Bernstein, whose 'Omnibus' programmes with the Symphony of the Air were winning Emmy Awards. If Bernstein were appointed, all that lucrative and wonderfully 'visible' employment would be enjoyed by the New York Philharmonic. Once again, Bernstein's timing was perfect!

Finally, when the announcement of Bernstein's sole assumption of responsibilities was made late in 1957, the orchestra formally listed the additional duties involved (which Rodzinski had demanded and Judson had so adamantly refused), all of which had been recommended in Howard Taubman's article.

The appointment of Leonard Bernstein was a significant moment in American musical history. He was the first home-grown artist to become musical director of an American orchestra in a country which had previously insisted upon European imports, and it is sometimes overlooked that, until as recently as 1958, no American musician had led any of the so-called 'Big Five' (New York, Boston, Philadelphia, Chicago and Cleveland), or most of the lesser orchestras. American musical life had been dominated by European conductors and European culture. The arrival of Bernstein, a native American trained in America, to head one of the great showcase organizations, gave his fellow musicians a new self-confidence and the realization that they had finally 'come of age'.

When Bernstein returned from Israel in November of 1957, he was joined by Mitropoulos for the press conference to announce his full appointment for the following season. If there were any hard feelings on the older man's part, he did not show them, saying only that he was happy to abdicate in favour of his protégé, which would allow him to concentrate on his 'mistress', the opera. He also noted that the appointment of Bernstein was a sign that America had 'grown up'. Strangely, this observation, which only reflected the truth of a situation that had continued far longer than it should have, was regarded by some as 'condescending'. If a criticism was implied, it was directed against the boards of all the major orchestras who had for years ignored native talent, often settling for imported artists with lesser skills.

It has been suggested that Bernstein started using a baton (his first was a gift, made of Israeli olive wood) to distance himself from Mitropoulos. In fact, his choice was made with few psychological undertones. While in Israel, he had hurt his back, slipping a disc, and the use of the stick greatly aided him when body movements caused pain. After New York hospital treatment in November, his back recovered, but he continued with the baton, which greatly reduced muscular stress.

Bernstein with Dimitri Mitropoulos, co-director of the New York Philharmonic, at the November 1957 press conference which announced that Bernstein would have sole direction of the orchestra the following season

Bernstein poses with his proud parents, following his first concert as music director of the New York Philharmonic, 2 October 1958.

Although appointed for the 1957–8 season, Bernstein's first appearance as joint conductor with Mitropoulos was not until January 1958. Forever superstitious – he now wore the pair of cuff-links that belonged to Koussevitzky, always kissing them before going onstage – he included works from his 1943 surprise début. This was followed two weeks later by the first televised Young People's Concert, a series he was to present for the next fourteen years.

The New York Philharmonic had run children's concerts for many years, but they had previously been assigned to other conductors (before Bernstein Wilfrid Pelletier had been in charge). Bernstein again displayed his gifts as a 'natural' teacher, writing his own material and presenting it in a simple, unpatronizing manner, using language that was immediately understood. Above all, while the programmes were entertaining and often amusing, involving the participation of his audience, he communicated serious musical messages – the meaning of music, the influence of folk origins, the structure of a fugue, what makes music symphonic – to children and parents alike. The live concerts played to packed houses and became a New York tradition. The televised programmes, in addition to reaching a large American audience, were shown in twenty-nine other countries, bringing Bernstein further international fame and, as Howard Taubman had proposed, putting the New York Philharmonic before the largest possible audience.

The final concert of the season, in the spring of 1958, gave Bernstein the opportunity to appear with Felicia, who spoke the role of Saint Joan in Honegger's oratorio *Jeanne d'Arc au Bûcher*. It was a great triumph, further establishing the Bernsteins as the most celebrated, sought-after fashionable couple in New York, and the toast of the town. Behind the scenes, Leonard was making wide-ranging plans and innovations for his first 'solo' season with the Philharmonic, but many of these had to be set aside when he left with the orchestra for a seven-week Latin American tour. His co-conductor Mitropoulos was completing engagements at the Metropolitan Opera and could not join the orchestra for about five weeks, leaving Bernstein to cover the initial concerts.

Bernstein toys with a weapon while admiring the colonial art collection of Pedro de Osma in Lima, Peru, during the New York Philharmonic's South American tour in Spring 1958.

The tour was part of a goodwill Presidential cultural mission, funded by Washington, and coincided with trips by Vice President Nixon, whose presence was clearly unwelcome to crowds filled with resentment for American exploitation of their countries. Bernstein and the orchestra were received with wild, Latin-American enthusiasm wherever they appeared, while the unfortunate Nixon party was greeted with boos, demonstrations and, occasionally, stones hurled at their motorcade. The tour was an exhilarating, if exhausting, experience for both conductors and gave Bernstein many informal opportunities, offered by being 'on the road' together, to renew acquaintance with individual members of the Philharmonic before the new season began in September. It also marked the start of yet another role in Bernstein's life: that of musical ambassador for his country.

After another summer at Martha's Vineyard, which included more revisions on *Candide* in preparation for the London production, Bernstein returned to New York to put into practice all his new plans for the orchestra. During the preceding February, he had already outlined an imaginative personal musical programme that would explore the works of American composers, from the earliest (and almost unknown) pioneers to the present day, combining them with standard orchestral fare, while guest conductors (in a list which included Mitropoulos and Herbert von Karajan) would perform standard and contemporary works of other countries.

The American series, divided into four segments, would create a fascinating survey. Early New England composers like George Chadwick (1854–1931) and Arthur Foote (1853–1937) would be followed by the more familiar Edward MacDowell and Charles Ives, whom Bernstein had already 'rediscovered' with enormous success. Gershwin and Copland would be included with Walter Piston and Randall Thompson (Bernstein's own teachers), and he added Samuel Barber, Paul Creston and – at last – Virgil Thomson. From his own generation, he chose Lukas Foss and Irving Fine, as well as younger composers like Ned Rorem and Gunther Schuller. Finally, to round off his first season, there would be a Handel Festival to mark the bicentenary of the composer's death.

It was an exciting start, but there was more to come. Thursday-night concerts (normally the first of the week's programme) were to be discontinued. In their place would be a new full-price subscription series called Preview Concerts, at which Bernstein (and any of his guests) could give a talk about the music or even stop the performance to discuss a point with the players or the audience. The concerts would resemble final dress rehearsals and, to emphasize the relaxed atmosphere of the occasion, the players would wear a specially designed costume, with high-sided collar and no lapels, that resembled the jackets that Toscanini and Bruno Walter had always worn at their rehearsals. In addition, the critics would not be invited and would have to content themselves with attending Friday afternoon matinées (usually dominated by wealthy New York society matrons, who rustled the pages of their magazines throughout the performance!).

The opening concert included William Schuman's *American Festival Overture*, Charles Ives's Second Symphony, and works by Beethoven and Berlioz. With more than a little help from the stylish and fashion-conscious Felicia, working with a fundraising group called Friends of the Philharmonic and various exclusive department stores (who were only too willing to oblige), it was a triumphantly festive evening in the grand Koussevitzky tradition. *Life* magazine covered the occasion, which was considered socially as well as musically one of *the* events of the season.

Bernstein had earlier admitted that everything he did had a touch of the theatrical to it and, in showbiz terms, the concert season was a smash hit. The critics were delighted, noting that the orchestra played with a tautness that had been missing. Howard Taubman, who always claimed that he had not considered Bernstein when writing his famous article, was nevertheless delighted with the results. He observed that the orchestra, in this first season, played 'with fresh pride and rediscovered coherence'. He also admired Bernstein's 'spirit of drive and curiosity, humour and sincerity'. The board of the Philharmonic could not have been happier. Subscriptions were rising rapidly, the orchestra was playing to full houses and the press was on their side. In addition, the musicians were earning higher wages, with handsome television fees thrown in and additional income from touring.

Not all of Bernstein's innovations were to be lasting. The rehearsal jackets designed for the Preview Concerts, unkindly dubbed 'Bernstein's Folly', were later discontinued and Bernstein returned to white tie and tails for the supposedly 'casual' series. (Guests such as

Herbert von Karajan and Sir John Barbirolli ignored such new-fangled fripperies.) Few of his guest conductors took the opportunity to speak, although Bernstein, who never interrupted a performance, continued to introduce his own programmes. Audiences from that era will remember with nostalgia his acute and often witty observations. In everything Bernstein undertook, he sought to *communicate* with his audiences, sharing his great love of music, even if it meant breaking down traditional barriers. He was not always successful, but at least he tried. Throughout his decade with the New York Philharmonic, each season was accompanied by a continuing theme and although Preview Concerts did not continue much beyond 1962, pre-concert talks have become an occasional practice for orchestras in many countries ever since.

Artur Rodzinski died in late November and Bernstein dedicated his concerts to him, paying tribute to the man who had appointed him as assistant in 1943 and given him his 'legendary' début. But in view of their stormy relationship and the periods of intense rivalry that followed, Bernstein's eloquent tribute – to close associates – must have sounded a little hollow.

Bernstein's first season with the Philharmonic was a triumph. He had taken time off, during appearances by guest conductors, to appear with great acclaim in both France and Italy, but decided thereafter to limit himself to his own orchestra for the duration of his contract. It was a popular move and may have been one of many reasons why the New York Philharmonic later extended his contract for a further seven years.

At the end of the season, Bernstein travelled with Felicia to London, where the critics, who had mostly been lukewarm in their reaction to *West Side Story*, were even less enthusiastic about (the revised) *Candide*, which still used Lillian Hellman's book, but had new costumes and décor by Osbert Lancaster. He returned to New York in time for the ground-breaking ceremonies for the Philharmonic Hall, which would be the first building at the new Lincoln Center for the Arts. The family took a well-earned rest on Martha's Vineyard, before returning to the city for summer concerts at Lewisohn Stadium, to be followed by a major tour that had arisen unexpectedly. Once again, fortune favoured Bernstein. The State Department, as part of President Eisenhower's Special International Program, had set up a

ten-week tour of Western Europe, the Middle East and the Soviet
Union for Fritz Reiner and the Chicago Symphony Orchestra. Much
to the irritation of his Chicago players, the seventy-year-old Reiner,
who had already suffered minor heart problems, cancelled the trip on
the grounds that it was too demanding. Bernstein and the
Philharmonic, assisted by the conductors Seymour Lipkin and
Thomas Schippers, were invited to replace them. It was an ideal
showpiece for the orchestra and once again established Bernstein as
America's principal musical ambassador. Their first seven concerts, in
Greece, Lebanon (without Bernstein, for political reasons) and Turkey
were played in open-air stadiums to rapturous audiences. From there,

On an extensive tour of
Western Europe in the
Autumn of 1959, Bernstein
conducts the New York
Philharmonic at the
amphitheatre in Athens.

they travelled to the Salzburg Festival, Warsaw and the Soviet Union, for eight concerts in Moscow, six in Leningrad and four in Kiev.

While America enjoyed the musical leadership of a number of major artists, the Western European music world was dominated by the presence of one conductor – Herbert von Karajan – who enjoyed the sort of respect and acclaim that only the legendary Arturo Toscanini had known in earlier years. Karajan was familiar to American audiences through his many recordings on EMI and DGG (and had been a guest of the New York Philharmonic when Bernstein first took over). He had also visited the United States in 1955 with the Berlin Philharmonic Orchestra, which he had inherited from Wilhelm Furtwängler. American concert-goers, however, many of whom were Jewish, took a more sanguine view of the Austrian conductor, who had joined the Nazi party in the 1930s and had spent the war years in Germany. Karajan became Artistic Director of the Salzburg Festival in 1956 and when, at the beginning of 1957, he also became Director of the Vienna State Opera, many believed that he had assumed the mantle of 'Generalmusikdirektor' of Europe.

Herbert von Karajan reigned supreme in Salzburg, his birthplace, and although a number of visiting conductors and orchestras were invited to take part at the annual summer festival, the Karajan camp went to some lengths to make sure that their leader would never be upstaged. In Austria, where music and politics are synonymous, Bernstein had his first taste of behind-the-scenes manipulation, when local Karajan minions, courting approval from their benevolent despot, tried to sabotage the New York Philharmonic's appearance by spreading rumours that there were no tickets available. Concierges at the local hotels – the normal source of supply – announced that the concert was already sold out when, in fact, few tickets had been taken. Carlos Mosely, the orchestra's Press Director, skilfully countered their efforts and ensured a full house. (At the reception hosted by the Vienna Philharmonic, the resident orchestra, Karajan was present to extend friendship and *gemütlichkeit*!)

In Warsaw, Bernstein made *ex officio* appearances at a local jazz club, and the orchestral concert in Congress Hall was such a success that the audience would not let him leave the stage until he had given an additional off-the-cuff solo piano recital. The climax of the tour came in Moscow, where Bernstein was hailed as a hero at the first

concert, which featured one of his 'showpiece' works, Shostakovich's
Fifth Symphony. Politics, however, started to intervene. At the second
concert, the Russians had not translated his long discourse on *The Age
of Anxiety* in the programme notes, and this, he felt, made the content
of the music difficult to follow. (Years later he admitted that the work
could be 'understood' without Auden's poem.) Then, following his
New York Preview pattern, he surprised – perhaps shocked – his
Russian audiences by introducing works with comments made via an
interpreter. At a concert that included Stravinsky's *Rite of Spring* and
Concerto for Piano and Wind Instruments, as well as *The
Unanswered Question* by Charles Ives, he observed that the Stravinsky
concerto had never been played and that the *Rite*, one of the pivotal
works of twentieth-century music, had not been heard in Russia for
thirty years. He added, more than tactlessly, that Stravinsky had
created a revolution five years before the Russians' own.

To be fair, a musician might regard the *Rite of Spring* as a shattering
moment in musical history but, whatever Russians may have felt
privately about life under Communism, it was gauche, if not
insulting, to compare reaction to Stravinsky's ballet with the rebirth of
their nation. Bernstein probably did not even realize the poor taste of
his remark. It simply indicates how much even he, as a liberal thinker
who despised McCarthyism and all it stood for, had been brain-
washed in the cold war of the 1950s.

He also explained Ives's revolutionary ideas, completely new to
Russian ears, and, when the audience cheered and stamped their
reaction to *The Unanswered Question*, repeated the performance.
Aleksandr Medvedev, the Cultural Ministry's music critic, was quick
to respond, attacking Bernstein for speaking to the audience, for
repeating the Ives, and for his 'show' called 'Leonard Bernstein Is
Lifting The Iron Curtain In Music'. It was all something of a storm in
a musical teacup, but Bernstein's words and actions helped clear the
path for Igor Stravinsky to make a triumphant return visit to the land
of his birth after many years of self-imposed exile.

Two other important non-musical events took place during this
historic tour. The first was a distressing reunion between Sam
Bernstein, persuaded against his will to join the family in Moscow,
and his younger brother whom he had not seen since he had made his
escape from Russia fifty years earlier. The men greeted one another

with emotional bear hugs, but then found that, across a political and cultural gulf of half a century, they had nothing to say to each other. The second, organized with a combination of determination and good fortune by Felicia, was a meeting with the great Russian writer, Boris Pasternak, the author of *Doctor Zhivago* and recipient of the Nobel Prize for Literature, which he had been forced to decline by the Russian authorities. The Bernsteins dined with the great Russian writer, and Pasternak also attended Bernstein's final Moscow concert, where he again conducted Shostakovich's Fifth Symphony, this time with the composer in the audience.

Despite Bernstein's diplomatic *faux pas*, the Russian tour had been a triumph and the orchestra completed the last leg of its trip in Western Europe, finishing in London, where the critics praised the New York Philharmonic but mostly savaged Bernstein's 'stunt' conducting and movements that looked as though they had been 'choreographed for him by Jerome Robbins'. The musical odyssey ended in Washington where, having arrived by air that morning, the orchestra gave a concert the same evening for an audience that included the ambassadors of all the countries they had visited.

At a press conference, Bernstein, who could never resist having the last word, criticized Russian music for its lack of experiment and re-hashing of outmoded systems. In retaliation, Shostakovich, Kabalevsky and Khachaturian published a joint letter in *Pravda*, denouncing Bernstein. He was possibly not fully aware of the rigorous controls under which Soviet composers worked. They, in turn, were hurt by his ungracious response to their hospitality and warmth.

For the new season Bernstein concentrated on the music of the Gustav Mahler, the composer with whom he would become deeply associated for the rest of his life, sharing a broad survey of the symphonies and orchestral songs with Dimitri Mitropoulos and Bruno Walter. (Bernstein eventually recorded all the symphonies for Columbia Records.) Other guest conductors included Fritz Reiner and Leopold Stokowski, and further programmes in the season would explore the history of the concerto and a festival of music for the theatre. Once again, the season was a huge artistic and financial success, and the Philharmonic reported increased subscriptions and box-office receipts. Bernstein, appearing frequently on television, had the drawing-power of a superstar, something rarely achieved by any orchestral conductor. In the spring of 1959, he had formed Amberson Enterprises to look after his wide-ranging financial and legal business and, together with the ever-faithful Helen Coates, who handled personal matters and the curatorship of a growing Bernstein 'archive', he was becoming an American institution.

Success, however, took its toll. By the spring of 1960, his health was poor: he was sleeping badly and living on nervous energy. Furthermore, he could not 'switch off' from all his public activities to turn his attention to composing, which he still saw as his primary function. *West Side Story* reopened on Broadway for a second run and, following an all too short holiday, Bernstein led the orchestra in another exhausting major American tour, continuing on to the 1960 Berlin Festival.

Carnegie Hall had been scheduled for destruction in 1960, to be replaced by an office building but, thanks to the work of Isaac Stern and others, the grand old concert hall with its superb acoustics was saved and Stern opened the new season in it with Beethoven's Violin Concerto. In November that year, Bernstein's first book, *The Joy of*

Bernstein talks to the Control Room during one of his many recording sessions for Columbia Records in New York, 6 January 1958.

Music, was published. Mostly a compilation of material used elsewhere (seven 'Omnibus' scripts, and articles reprinted from the *New York Times* and *Atlantic Monthly* magazine), it also contained three humorous 'conversations', discussing subjects as diverse as the Great American Symphony and what makes a Broadway hit. The book was an instant bestseller, listed for months, and was translated into many languages.

November was also a month of contrasting emotions. Bernstein's friend Senator John F. Kennedy was elected President, and during that golden era the Bernsteins would become regular visitors to the White House. On 27 November Dimitri Mitropoulos died, collapsing during a rehearsal of Mahler's Third Symphony at La Scala, Milan. In a tribute concert, Bernstein conducted the fourth (*Urlicht*) movement of the Second Symphony, the solo part sung by Jennie Tourel, and undertook to conduct the entire work, which Mitropoulos had been scheduled to perform, later in the season.

In February 1961, at a gala 'Valentine for Leonard Bernstein' (who had just renewed his contract for a further seven years), the orchestra, conducted by Lukas Foss, gave the first performance of the Symphonic Dances from *West Side Story*. All the music comes from the original show, but the order is slightly changed to suit the concert hall. The original orchestration of the Broadway show, by Irwin Kostal and Sid Ramin, had been undertaken under Bernstein's supervision (and both Kostal and Ramin had expressed enormous admiration for his skills, making it clear that their work was only an extension of the composer, who was simply too busy to undertake all the writing himself in the run-up to the show). The score for this suite again makes use of Kostal and Ramin's orchestrations, supervised by Bernstein and extended to take advantage of a full symphony orchestra.

Jack Gottlieb, who first began to work as Bernstein's assistant in 1958, and who has been his most articulate and authoritative annotator ever since, has pointed out that *West Side Story* is an original theatrical conception, fusing European and American musical elements to create a work that is neither opera nor musical comedy. The dances in the suite are labelled 'symphonic' because they were conceived as such even for the stage presentation. (That is to say, although the music in the show is an accompaniment to the dancers,

THE HENLEY COLLEGE LIBRARY

Bernstein originally composed it as dramatic incidental music, irrespective of choreography, almost as Bizet composed dramatic incidental music to the play *L'Arlésienne*.) Gottlieb adds that they were also conceived as an 'organic self-contained whole' that can be appreciated without knowledge of the action taking place on the stage. The work is in nine sections, played without pause; it makes use of material exclusively written for the show and, while its melodies and rhythms (alternately haunting or dazzling) may recall dramatic moments from the original, it can – rather like the Symphonic Suite from *On the Waterfront* – be enjoyed for the sheer musical power and pleasure it conveys. It has become one of Bernstein's most performed works for the concert hall, delighting audiences who could well be young enough never to have seen either the stage production or the film, which was released with enormous international success in October of the same year.

The 1960–61 season marked a change in Bernstein's fortunes with the music press. Howard Taubman, Bernstein's champion since his appointment, moved to the drama department of the *New York Times*, to be replaced by Harold Schonberg, a dedicated, knowledgeable but conservative critic, who objected to Bernstein's podium histrionics, was critical of his overheated interpretations, disliked the manner in which he upstaged his soloists, and called for good musicianship to replace Bernstein's 'showbiz' exhibitionism. In 1959, he had ridiculed the Preview Concert uniforms, and he would later subject the pianist

Leonard Bernstein (left) with the pianist Glenn Gould (centre) and composer Igor Stravinsky; on 31 January 1960 Stravinsky and Gould appeared on television with Bernstein as part of the series 'Leonard Bernstein and the New York Philharmonic'.

A scene from the film of *West Side Story*; the film's enormous success helped establish Bernstein's international reputation with a non-classical music audience.

Glenn Gould to merciless criticism, laced with acerbic humour, for an eccentric performance of the Brahms D minor Concerto, which Bernstein had directed. Schonberg was not alone, and although the Philharmonic's board was satisfied with its Music Director, there was a sense of growing unease in the critical community. Bernstein did nothing to change or 'mend' his ways (and it is more than likely that he could not have changed them; his podium 'eccentricities' were totally honest), but admitted in later years that the constant sniping of the New York critics had hurt him at the time. Like many highly sensitive, creative men, he sought – in fact, needed – constant encouragement.

In April and May of 1961, Bernstein went to Japan with the orchestra. He was enchanted by the country's oriental charms, but his audiences, raised in the strictly restrained European tradition (epitomized by Karajan), were initially hesitant to accept his extrovert music-making. He steadily endeared himself with audiences, however, learning enough of the language from his youthful assistant Seiji Ozawa to address them in Japanese. Ozawa was a Koussevitzky Award winner from Tanglewood, and Bernstein earned great acclaim when he publicly invited his talented protégé to conduct a work by the Japanese composer Toshirō Mayuzumi.

The Japanese conductor Seiji Ozawa, an assistant of Bernstein's at the New York Philharmonic, and one of his numerous protégés

Bernstein's last work composed for the concert hall, the violin *Serenade*, had been written in 1954. Eight years later, at the beginning of 1962, he was considering a deeply serious new work, which would become his controversial Third Symphony (*Kaddish*). Humphrey Burton notes that the work was already taking shape in Bernstein's thoughts when he helped celebrate his father's seventieth birthday in January of that year. He spoke about the links between a father and his son, at times likening it to the relationship between man and God, and discussing in particular the moment when every son defies his father, hopefully to return to him feeling closer and more secure than before. Bernstein's relationship with his father had been unhappy during his youth, and when he had first achieved success in the early 1940s, he could not resist publicly attacking his father for having tried to block his musical career. There had been other bitter moments, and Sam Bernstein must have been wounded when his son had chosen the name Sam for the ruthlessly ambitious anti-hero of *Trouble in Tahiti*. But, Leonard himself was about to become a father again and, admitting that parenthood had given him a better understanding of his own father, he remembered an early effort at composition, and entertained the guests by playing a new variation called 'Meditation on a Prayerful Theme My Father Sang in the Shower Thirty Years Ago'. It later found its way into the new symphony. The following month, Felicia gave birth to their third child, Nina Maria Felicia.

At the end of the season (which had included the *affaire* Gould), he completed his television commitments and, after more work on the symphony, took Felicia on a long-promised holiday that included a

Leonard and Felicia
Bernstein, the most glamorous
couple in New York

Mediterranean cruise, conducting Prince Rainier's orchestra in Monaco, and ten days in Spain.

In September, he conducted the inaugural concert of the new Philharmonic Hall at Lincoln Center. It was a mixed bag of a programme, ranging from the Gloria of Beethoven's *Missa solemnis*, the *Serenade to Music* by Vaughan Williams and the first movement of Mahler's Eighth Symphony, to Aaron Copland's craggy *Connotations*, a work commissioned for the celebrations surrounding the opening of the new hall. It had been hoped that the President would attend the opening, but Kennedy stayed away, according to some sources, because he was irritated by Bernstein's alliance with those protesting against the build-up of nuclear arsenals, which led him to take part in a march on Washington led by Harry Belafonte and Helen Gahagan Douglas. The President's wife, Jacqueline Kennedy, did come to the first half of the concert, and television viewers nationwide were slightly taken aback when a shiny-faced Bernstein, meeting her backstage during the intermission, cheerfully announced 'I'm all sweated up', and planted an uninvited kiss on the First Lady's cheek. (Years later, in an interview, she dismissed the idea that she had been upset by such *lèse majesté*.)

The new hall at Lincoln Center, while it looked elegant from the outside and enjoyed air-conditioning inside, could not match the acoustics of Carnegie Hall, but Bernstein struggled on, defending it against all-comers, while privately demanding work to improve the unattractive sound of the auditorium. (The hall was later redesigned at enormous expense, and some wag suggested that Isaac Stern should play concerts to save it, as he had for Carnegie Hall!) The 1962–3 season featured a number of premières, composed for the first season in the new venue, including Poulenc's *Sept Répons des ténèbres*, with an embarrassingly anti-Semitic Biblical text concerning the death of Christ that dismayed many of the Philharmonic's Jewish subscribers.

Bernstein was working steadily on *Kaddish*, despite the constant interruptions and distractions that his role at the Philharmonic demanded. Felicia was called away to her mother's death-bed in Santiago, but he was unable to join her because the orchestra's season was not completed. In addition, the family moved into their new Connecticut home in June, and there were recording sessions and numerous conferences concerning the acoustics of the new hall, as

Bernstein meets the London press; the enthusiastic photographic response was such that the press corps needed to be almost forcibly removed.

well as plans for the following seasons to be made. His new work called for a narration (which Felicia would speak) and, following unsuccessful discussions with several writers including the poet Robert Lowell, Bernstein decided to write the text himself.

Originally commissioned by the Koussevitzky Foundation in 1955 – when Charles Munch was the music director of the Boston Symphony – the symphony was already some years late, and Munch now asked if it could at least be ready by January of 1964, when he would be a guest conductor with the orchestra. Bernstein worked hard into the summer of 1963, and completed writing, but not orchestrating, the symphony in mid August.

On Friday 22 November 1963, a date which haunts the memory of all Americans, Bernstein was at Philharmonic Hall, preparing a Young People's Concert, when the news of President Kennedy's assassination was reported. On the Sunday evening, he conducted a performance of Mahler's Second Symphony ('The Resurrection') on television. He had already decided to dedicate his new *Kaddish* symphony 'To the beloved memory of John F. Kennedy'.

Because of the Jewish nature of the work (*Kaddish* is both a prayer glorifying God, recited at the end of a synagogue service, and also the prayer that children recite at the graves of their parents), Bernstein sought permission to give the first performance of the work in Israel, and the Boston Symphony (as Koussevitzky had done with *Peter Grimes*) waived its first-performance right. Concerned that the controversial nature of the text might cause offense, Bernstein contacted the Israel Philharmonic, offering to withdraw the work if it would cause problems. Abe Cohen, the orchestra's manager, reassured him that experts on Hebrew literature and philosophy had found nothing offensive in the text, adding that similar precedents already existed. The words were then translated into Hebrew, and the first performance, spoken by the renowned Israeli classical actress Hannah Rovina, and with Jennie Tourel singing the solo soprano role, was conducted in Tel Aviv by Bernstein on 10 December 1963.

Although *kaddish* is said for the dead, the word 'death' is never mentioned and the prayer is an affirmation of life, praising the name of God and hoping for everlasting peace. It is spoken in two languages: Aramaic (the vernacular language that dates from the time of Jesus and his followers) and – in the call for peace – Biblical Hebrew. In the symphony, this prayer is sung three times: the first time, anguished; the second, as a peaceful lullaby for soprano and female choir; the third, jubilant. Binding the three together is a Speaker, who introduces the first *kaddish* with an *Invocation*, calling upon God to listen. The *kaddish* is followed by a *Din-Torah* (or 'Trial by God's Law') in which the Speaker angrily reproaches God for forsaking mankind, accusing Him of withdrawing hope. Then, apologizing for such an outburst, the Speaker introduces the second *kaddish* – the lullaby – which offers God comfort for His disappointment in His creatures. This is followed by the most critical point, dramatically and musically, of the work: a Scherzo, in which the Speaker mentally reverses roles with God, to persuade Him to renew His faith in man. A jubilant boys' choir introduces the third *kaddish*. The dream ends, and a new, wiser person emerges, reborn at peace with God and with faith restored and renewed. The work is performed without a break.

The text, written at a time when fingers hovered over nuclear buttons of destruction, reveals the underlying darkness of cold war times. In the *Invocation*, one hears 'Is my end a minute away? An hour?' Later, the Speaker harangues God for deserting man, allowing him 'to play with his new-found fire, avid for death'. The killing of President Kennedy and, on a broader scale, the survival of humanity, were Bernstein's prevailing troubled thoughts during that period. The need for faith was a theme that had inspired both *Jeremiah* and *The Age of Anxiety*, and *Kaddish* was a prayer offered on behalf of everyone.

When preparing his text, Bernstein never intended to be blasphemous. Indeed, Hebrew tradition has always accepted that philosophers searching for truths may find them by disputing with God. This was particularly true in the breakaway Hasidic movement, a sect to which Bernstein's father had belonged. (At one time Bernstein considered writing an opera about the false Messiahs who had appeared during the eighteenth century.) In his notes to the first recording of *Kaddish*, Jack Gottlieb refers to Bernstein's feelings for the 'peculiar Jewishness of this man–God relationship … which allows things to be said to God that are almost inconceivable in another religion.'

Musically, Bernstein's score underlines the character of the text, the anguish and despair reflected in the music's dissonance slowly giving way to an ordered and peacefully resolved tonality. Throughout his composing life, he fought against the demands of twelve-tone music and the mathematical tyranny of the followers of Arnold Schoenberg and the Second Viennese School, even when it was fashionable to join their élitist club. In the post-serial era of the 1990s, Bernstein now appears to have been a voice in the wilderness and a prophet in his time.

The next performances of the symphony, narrated in English by Felicia Montealegre, were given by Munch in Boston, as promised. The reviews were very mixed, attacking Bernstein for 'vulgarity', 'clichés' and derivative music. (The finale of the work does bear a strong melodic similarity to a theme in Copland's *Appalachian Spring*, but such phenomena often occur unintentionally, despite the theories of self-elected musical 'detectives'.) The critiques were not all bad. Harold Rogers of the *Christian Science Monitor* (one of America's most distinguished newspapers) described it as 'the composer at his most serious and his finest'. In New York, there was the same mixture of praise and vitriol, except that the bad reviews seemed to contain a greater degree of personal attack. The *New York World Telegram* and *Sun*'s reviewer, Louis Biancolli, who had nearly always supported Bernstein, wrote that 'a giant pulse of integrity throbs through it', but Alan Rich of the *Herald-Tribune* suggested that the name *Kaddish* could well be replaced by the title *Chutzpah*. *Time* magazine wrote that Bernstein's was 'the despair of the prideful', and by and large this was the fate that the symphony and its composer suffered at the time. There was an air of 'who does he think he is?' in the negative reviews, as though Bernstein's critics were still shaking their heads at the sight of the bumptious conductor of the New York Philharmonic planting a sweaty kiss on the cheek of the First Lady. Worse still, according to Rich, he was now telling off God in no uncertain terms.

Kaddish is one of Leonard Bernstein's finest works, and probably deserves the sobriquet 'masterpiece'. It is also his least understood and, consequently, least performed music, and one can only hope that time and re-evaluation will correct such oversights. Structurally, musically and philosophically, it succeeds as an artistic *chef-d'œuvre* but, like many important works of art, it was ahead of its time, and its critics were too busy attacking its composer to recognize the quality of his creation.

Despite many endearing qualities, which included love, friendship, loyalty and generosity, there is little question that, throughout his musical career, Bernstein was at times arrogant, self-serving, attention-seeking and egotistical. Such character flaws should not influence critical judgement of his work as a composer. While the representation of Mozart in the play *Amadeus* is a gross distortion of the real person, there is also little doubt that Wolfgang Amadeus could be an extremely unattractive and precocious *enfant terrible*. History has shown, however, that he was one of the greatest composers of any era and judgement of his music has never been coloured by his failings as a human being. This is not to suggest that Leonard Bernstein should be placed on the same pedestal as Mozart, or even that his music should be mentioned in the same breath; only that Bernstein's works must be judged for themselves and not for the character of their creator.

Bernstein later modified and slightly reduced the text of *Kaddish* so that it could be spoken by a man or a woman, and made a few musical changes, which he felt tightened the whole work, while leaving it 'essentially the same'. More than thirty years after its première, it remains a powerfully convincing work and, removed from the personal presence of its composer, its message is equally strong. It was perhaps the highly dramatic treatment of a deeply religious subject that angered his most virulent critics, but Bernstein had already given warning fourteen years earlier, in his introductory notes to *The Age of Anxiety*, that everything he wrote was really music for the theatre.

His next venture took him to the theatre: in this case, to the Metropolitan Opera for a sparkling new production of Verdi's *Falstaff*, directed by Franco Zeffirelli. It was an ideal partnership with the brilliant Italian director, and they created a witty and masterly presentation for the old Metropolitan house before it was demolished in favour of the new building being erected at Lincoln Center. Bernstein had just suffered week after week of critical mauling for a badly conceived and poorly presented Philharmonic series that tried unsuccessfully to sandwich avant-garde works between standard orchestral favourites (composers like György Ligeti and Iannis Xenakis in-between Beethoven and Saint-Saëns), thereby alienating both press and public. He now had the satisfaction of reading newspapers full of glowing reviews, with even Harold Schonberg favourably impressed.

The Philharmonic's 1964–5 season was to be a sabbatical, with the exception of the ever-popular Young People's Concerts, because Bernstein, once his creative powers had been focused, was eager to return to composing. His main project was to be a musical adaptation of Thornton Wilder's tragicomedy *The Skin of our Teeth*, in which the author of *Our Town* had written an allegory of the history of mankind 'in comic strip'. His partners would be Comden and Green, with direction and choreography again by Jerome Robbins, but his collaboration with this seemingly indestructible team failed to produce a tangible result, and the second half of 1964 was, for him, distressingly 'wasted'. This is, of course, a slight exaggeration. Even when Bernstein was not occupied with the business of heading the Philharmonic, he was constantly in demand and fulfilled many engagements that were required of a public figure of his stature.

By early 1965, however, he was still without a project on which to work. He had rarely composed in a programmatic vacuum, and needed a 'theme' to inspire his writing, even if the final work would

survive independently of the idea that motivated it. Fortunately, help arrived from an unexpected quarter. Every summer, the choirs of the English cathedrals of Winchester, Salisbury and Chichester joined forces for a music festival. For the 1965 festival, the Very Reverend Walter Hussey, Dean of Chichester Cathedral, wrote to Bernstein, offering him the commission of a new choral work. His timing happened to be perfect. If Bernstein had been preoccupied successfully with another project, he might have accepted Dr Hussey's invitation only to leave it to wait for years, as in the case of *Kaddish*. Instead, he set to work almost immediately. Quite charmingly, the Dean warned Bernstein (who had just completed *Kaddish* for a massive orchestra) that for reasons of space and expense, it would not be possible to have a full symphony orchestra, but added that 'a hint of *West Side Story*' in the new piece would be welcomed!

The resulting *Chichester Psalms* is one of Leonard Bernstein's most popular and immediately accessible works. Like *Kaddish*, its text is in Hebrew, but while the earlier work expresses despair resolving into hope for the future, the *Psalms* are filled with joy and absolute trust in God. There are no arguments or angry accusations. Starting with Psalm 108 ('Awake, psaltery and harp! I will rouse the dawn'), it continues with the complete Psalm 100 ('Make a joyful noise unto the Lord all ye lands'). The second movement opens with the favourite Psalm 23 ('The Lord is my shepherd, I shall not want') sung by a boy alto, suggesting King David as a shepherd-boy, but is interrupted by the men's choir, singing verses from Psalm 2 ('Why do the nations rage, and the people imagine a vain thing?'). The third and final movement opens with an orchestral 'meditation' which leads to a reassuring mood of comfort that combines Psalm 131 ('Lord, Lord, my heart is not haughty …') with the familiar opening of the serene Psalm 133 ('Behold how good and how pleasant it is for brethren to dwell together in unity').

Bernstein later referred to his 1964–5 sabbatical year as a period in which he had worked with twelve-tone music and other experimental forms, but had set them aside because such music was not *his* music; it was not honest. He added that if one is looking for optimism versus pessimism in his music, 'the closest musical equivalent is tonality versus non-tonality.' He described *Chichester Psalms* as 'the most accessible, B-flat-majorish tonal piece I've ever written'. It is also one

Opposite, the Young People's Concerts attracted fans of all ages.

of his most touchingly beautiful works, with a freshness and sweetness which are renewed with every performance. It belongs among the finest choral pieces of this century.

Dr Hussey was delighted with Bernstein's work, adding that he was proud to think of the *Psalms* going round the world bearing the name of Chichester. His 'hint of *West Side Story*' appears in 'Why do the nations …' of the second movement, which is a reworking of a prologue written for the Broadway show, but not used. (In addition, Bernstein was able to salvage some of the thematic material he had composed for the discarded *Skin of our Teeth*.) Bernstein obtained permission from Chichester to give his work a 'try-out' in New York in July 1965, before the world première in Chichester. It was extemely well received, accompanied by friendly, positive reviews. But the British press, which had still not warmed to Bernstein, remained very mixed.

When he returned to the New York Philharmonic in the autumn, it was to begin an ambitious two-year survey of twentieth-century symphonic forms, with special emphasis on the works of Mahler. Backed by his record company, it was a wide-ranging programme and one which would place him at the forefront of American music-making.

The public adored him. With the success of his Broadway shows and with fascinating television programmes that made 'serious' music interesting even for the uninitiated, he had proved that 'long-hair' entertainment need not be dull or 'arty', and that classical musicians could be as witty, approachable and understandable as popular entertainers. His standing with the musicians in the orchestra could not have been higher. First, and most important, he brought them greater income, from extra television and recording work to extended tours and a longer season, than they had ever previously enjoyed. In addition, he had shown that it was possible to be democratic and to coax fine performances from players without necessarily resorting to the parade-ground discipline or histrionic tantrums of a Rodzinski or a Toscanini.

The only group which remained apparently impervious to Bernstein's charms was the press, although it must be pointed out that Harold Schonberg, who could be cruelly sarcastic when he was dissatisfied, was seldom totally unfair and, in Bernstein's last years as Music Director of the Philharmonic, became a somewhat grudging

Jacqueline Kennedy joins the Bernsteins for a concert of his songs.

supporter. The attacks passed from Schonberg in the *Times* to Alan Rich in the *Herald-Tribune*, who now chose Bernstein the composer as his target.

It may well have been his failure to win over the New York press that made Bernstein look further afield, or it could simply have been the realization that there was a much larger world than the blasé, somewhat insular musical confines of Manhattan. He loved his New York orchestra and, true to his word, had probably been more faithful to it than to his wife. For some years he had restricted his conducting to the New York and Israel Philharmonic orchestras, but his successful appearances at the Metropolitan Opera in the spring of 1964 reopened the door to theatre music. Early in 1966 he returned to Vienna, after an absence of eight years, to make his first appearance with the State Opera in a new production of Verdi's *Falstaff*, directed by Luchino Visconti, whom he had befriended in the heady Callas era, and starring Dietrich Fischer-Dieskau.

Despite certain psychological hesitations, prompted by Austria's active participation in Hitler's rise to power, it was love at first rehearsal, and Bernstein found himself welcomed, revered and, once the audience had heard him, adopted by the city which still saw itself as the centre of the music world and the cradle of Western music. The press, too, were unreservedly enthusiastic, in newspapers that were accustomed to dedicating four pages daily to musical subjects. If New Yorkers were often isolated from the rest of the active music world, the Viennese were also living in a stylish, old-fashioned world of their own, but it was a world of tradition and elegant living, with a musical history of Mozart, Beethoven, Schubert and a host of others, including Gustav Mahler. Furthermore, Vienna has a small, inward-looking musical community and for Bernstein, who had become the instant toast of the town, it was like living in a dream fulfilled.

Falstaff was recorded, and Bernstein went on to conduct concerts with the Vienna Philharmonic (which is made up of players from the State Opera orchestra). The performances served only to confirm the critical endorsement that had greeted the opera. In just five weeks,

Bernstein directs from the keyboard in a recital by players of the Vienna Philharmonic in Vienna's Schönbrunn Palace, 14 April 1966.

Bernstein had conquered Vienna and, perhaps even more significant in a city which frequently leaves its real motives unspoken, he had filled the gap left by Herbert von Karajan when he resigned from the State Opera in 1964.

From Vienna, Bernstein, accompanied by Felicia (who had joined him for the last *Falstaff* performance), flew to London. Ernest Fleischmann, the manager of the London Symphony Orchestra, had invited him to conduct Mahler's Seventh and gigantic Eighth ('Symphony of a Thousand') symphonies, also recording the latter at choral and orchestral rates that were were substantially lower than in America. The BBC televised the concert, which was played in the Royal Albert Hall.

After an absence from New York of only eight weeks (but they had been triumphal if extremely tiring weeks), Bernstein returned to complete the Philharmonic's season, which included the première of his old friend David Diamond's Fifth Symphony. New York must have seemed something of an anti-climax after the heady celebrations in Vienna, but he was welcomed home by friendlier reviews, including the famous comment by Harold Schonberg that if he continued to develop into the extraordinary musician that his talents had always indicated, 'musicians will call him "Maestro" instead of "Lenny"!'

In June, it was announced that Jacqueline Kennedy had persuaded Bernstein to write a work for the 1969 inauguration of the new Kennedy Center in Washington DC, at which he would also officiate as Artistic Director. In July, *Candide* reappeared, this time in a new revision in Los Angeles, directed by Gordon Davidson and conducted by Maurice Peress, who had been an assistant of Bernstein's in 1961. Bernstein took part in the preparations, offering encouragement and advice, and the production, which emphasized the satirical aspects of the original show, was well received. The following month, Bernstein's second book, *The Infinite Variety of Music*, was published. Apart from a striking essay on the creative process and analyses of several famous symphonies, it contained the scripts of five of his best television shows. It makes good reading, but is essentially a reworking of earlier material.

Once again, it was apparent that Bernstein the creative artist had completed an exhausting season as Bernstein the performer. The summer break was all too short before he returned to what he called 'the salt mines': a new season with the Philharmonic. His sabbatical year, during which a lot of time (and money) had been invested in *The Skin of our Teeth*, had in many ways been wasted, and the conducting schedule that he set himself did not allow enough time to unwind and settle down to the serious business of composing.

This is not the whole truth. Bernstein was never a dedicated full-time composer who, like Samuel Barber, went to his 'office' every morning and worked consistently (usually throwing most of the material in the waste-basket by the end of the day). Bernstein worked hard and played hard, relaxing with friends and enjoying life whenever he had periods of free time. He was easily distracted, was usually at his best when facing a deadline and could never have survived the self-imposed discipline that, for example, made Mahler withdraw from the world. If writing did not come naturally and quickly, as in the case of *Chichester Psalms*, he was an expert prevaricator and would latch on to any excuse to avoid getting on with the job.

Nevertheless, insisting that he was a frustrated composer, he advised the board of the New York Philharmonic that, apart from the Young People's Concerts, he would not renew his contract after May 1969. He would be happy to appear as a guest conductor and to continue to record with the orchestra, but he sought to be released from the further administrative duties and responsibilities for which Artur Rodzinski had battled so many years earlier. Several important events would still take place before his departure, including his own fiftieth birthday and the 1967–8 season marking the 125th anniversary of the orchestra. The board had no alternative but to accept Bernstein's withdrawal, but in gratitude for his oustanding services both to music and to the New York Philharmonic, created the new title, lifetime Laureate Conductor, to take effect from the end of the 1969 season.

In his farewell statement, made somewhat prematurely two and a half years before his departure, Bernstein stated his regret at leaving an orchestra and an organization that he had come to love, but that he 'must concentrate maximally on composing'. It is probable that the word 'maximally' was, even when he used it, an exaggeration. It is also probable that new-found friends and homes in Europe offered an attractive alternative to New York's hard-boiled press corps.

The 1966–7 season in the Philharmonic 'salt mines' was highlighted by a number of successes, including the début of the cellist Jacqueline du Pré and a performance of Mahler's Sixth Symphony which, for once, received unanimous critical acclaim. (The press were a great deal less enthusiastic about a television 'special' he presented for CBS, called 'Inside Pop – The Rock Revolution', in which he praised the invention and vitality of popular music when compared with the academic sterility of current classical experiments.) Bernstein had also spent some time mid-season working with the London Symphony Orchestra in concerts that were televised, establishing stronger links for future work with European orchestral organizations.

When the season ended, the Bernsteins planned a holiday in Italy during which they would be photographed by Ken Heyman and interviewed by John Gruen for an 'authorized biography' which would appear the following year to coincide with Bernstein's fiftieth birthday. John Gruen's wife, the artist Jane Wilson, would also be there to help Felicia, who had become interested in painting. (The book, entitled *The Private World of Leonard Bernstein*, proved to be a somewhat sycophantic coffee-table production. It earned the Bernsteins a few sarcastic sideswipes in the press and had little to do with serious biography.) Taking advantage of the Italian trip, Bernstein also agreed to some concert appearances in Florence and Rome.

While they were in Italy, the six-day war broke out in the Middle East. Bernstein conducted Mahler's 'Resurrection' Symphony in Vienna and donated his fee to the Israeli Red Cross, whereupon his soloists, Hilde Güden and Christa Ludwig, as well as all the members of the Vienna Philharmonic Orchestra, donated theirs. Later, after appearances at the first Lincoln Center Festival in New York, he flew to Israel to conduct concerts marking the peaceful reunification of Jerusalem. The trip was the subject of a documentary film called *Journey to Jerusalem*. As a grand finale to his visit, Bernstein conducted an outdoor concert at the Mount Scopus amphitheatre, at which the violinist Isaac Stern, Jennie Tourel and the distinguished Israeli soprano Netania Davrath took part. For Jews everywhere, these were stirring times and Bernstein was present to offer artistic leadership and cultural support.

At the end of an inspiring tour, he rejoined his family in Italy for a relaxed (but unproductive) holiday. Interview sessions with Gruen during the holiday were interspersed with visits from friends and a

constant round of entertainment. If, Mahler-like, Bernstein had
hoped that the period would be musically creative, he had chosen the
wrong place and made his presence there much too public. He
suffered from insomnia, was diverted by 'toys' (a new Maserati sports
car and the latest in diving equipment), went sight-seeing and, feeling
guilty and increasingly depressed, wrote nothing. His general sense of
gloom was underlined in an article, 'Mahler – His Time Has Come',
written for the magazine *High Fidelity* and also as an introduction to a
boxed set of the complete symphonies on record. In it, he listed all the
depressing events the world had witnessed between Mahler's death in
1911 and the present, suggesting that the composer's music could only
now be understood because it foretold the horrors of half a century in
'a rain of beauty'.

The New York Philharmonic's 1967–8 season was also its 125th
anniversary and the orchestra had commissioned twenty-five
composers to write new works as part of its celebrations. The Vienna
Philharmonic was sharing the same anniversary, and Karl Böhm and
Bernstein divided the honours. To open the new season, Bernstein
conducted the Viennese musicians and, the following week, Böhm
directed the New Yorkers. Bernstein also asserted his newly acquired
'Viennese' personality with a televised Young Person's Concert salute
to the city 'in 3/4 Time'.

The festivities renewed Bernstein's long-lasting friendship with
Aaron Copland, whose serial composition *Inscape* was one of the
many new commissions, and the conductor noted (with joy) that
Copland's music, even when subjected to the discipline of the twelve-
tone system, still *sounded* like Copland! In December, the New York
orchestra celebrated the actual anniversary by repeating its first
programme in a curious serendipity of works: a piano quintet by
Hummel, Beethoven's Fifth Symphony, arias by Weber, Mozart and
Beethoven, and an overture by Johann Kalliwoda (1801–66), a late
Classical/early Romantic Bohemian composer, whose tuneful but
somewhat lightweight music had apparently found favour with New
York concert-goers in 1842.

At the end of a highly successful season, during which Bernstein
earned a major share of the credit for the high standards and restored
qualities of the orchestra, he travelled to his new 'home' Vienna. He
was to conduct *Der Rosenkavalier*, the work most associated with that

city and so familiar to its audiences that most of them could have sung along with the cast. Unfortunately, it was also so routine for the musicians at the opera house that they took Richard Strauss's great score for granted and, in a manner which has been compared with restoring an Old Master, Bernstein persuaded the players to renew their acquaintance with the music. He re-seated the orchestra in the pit, re-bowed the string parts, tightened up the rhythms and removed some of the lazy habits that had crept into the playing after years of easy-going routine performances. The results were dazzling and Bernstein was again hailed as the new champion. During his month in Vienna, he conducted the Vienna Philharmonic, played the piano for Christa Ludwig and Walter Berry in a recital of Mahler songs and attended a performance at the Volksoper of *West Side Story*, translated into German by his friend Marcel Prawy. He was even offered the role of artistic director of the State Opera, the post that Mahler himself had held for a decade, but Bernstein turned it down because he wanted more time to compose.

His month in the Austrian capital had established him as a major Viennese attraction and, whether or not he had done so musically, he had replaced Herbert von Karajan emotionally in people's affections. They loved Bernstein, finding him far friendlier and more approachable than his imperious predecessor, and were charmed by his 'American' lack of formality. The feeling was mutual. Welcomed by an enthusiastic press, and captivated by Vienna's famed old-world lifestyle and traditions, Bernstein responded with open-hearted warmth. It is interesting to note that, on his return to New York, where he conducted a concert performance of the first act of Wagner's *Die Walküre*, his reading was compared with Karajan's performance of the complete opera, which had been imported from Salzburg by the Metropolitan Opera. Schonberg reported that Karajan's approach had been 'as much Karajan as Wagner', whereas Bernstein's was 'brilliant', adding that this was 'the way Wagner should sound … Mr Bernstein's avoidance of artificial effects was testimony to his continued growth as a musician.' This was praise indeed from a critic who had complained for years that everything Bernstein did was for personal effect.

If Schonberg's review gave him any joy, it was shattered within days by the news of Robert Kennedy's assassination. At the request of Jacqueline Kennedy, Bernstein supervised music for the funeral at St

Patrick's Cathedral in New York. He chose the Adagietto movement from Mahler's Fifth Symphony and the finale from Verdi's Requiem, for soprano and female voices. He was advised, however, that the latter piece would not be permitted because St Patrick's did not allow women's voices. Ethel Kennedy, Robert's widow, also requested songs from her youth, sung by the nuns of Manhattanville school, as well as *The Battle Hymn of the Republic* to be performed (this time against Bernstein's wishes) by the popular singer Andy Williams. To Bernstein's surprise, the Kennedy name carried a great deal more weight than his own when dealing with the monsignors of St Patrick's, and all the requests were granted. To his further surprise, the lone voice of Williams, singing the familiar words of the *Battle Hymn*, was an outstanding and touching moment in the service.

In the summer of 1968, Bernstein returned at last to composing, working on a musical adaptation, suggested by Jerome Robbins, of Bertold Brecht's *The Exception and the Rule*. It never saw completion, although Bernstein would return to it several more times. In August, having celebrated his fiftieth birthday (slightly in advance) with his family, he led the Philharmonic in an exhaustive tour of Western Europe and of Israel, their first visit there. Felicia, who was working actively on behalf of Senator Eugene McCarthy's Presidential campaign, did not accompany them. (The senator, who favoured a pacifist policy strongly endorsed by the Bernsteins, failed to achieve nomination at the Chicago Democratic convention, and they – and the rest of the world – watched with horror as peaceful demonstrations were met with Chicago Mayor Daly's police brutality.)

Bernstein's programmes for his final season as Music Director of the Philharmonic took the form of a retrospective survey of the music they had shared together over a decade. In October, he appeared with Fischer-Dieskau, both at the Philharmonic and in a fund-raising concert for UNICEF. In November, the publication of *The Private World of Leonard Bernstein* was dismissed by the critics, who treated it mostly as a piece of self-promotional public relations with insider-style 'happy family' pictures. Richard Rodzinski, the conductor's son, complained to the *New York Times* that Bernstein should not have revealed the fact that his hot-tempered father had once grabbed him by the throat and threatened to throttle him. Over the years, Bernstein's less attractive behaviour could have inspired any number of others to emulate Rodzinski, who had treated his protégé generously in supporting his historic début. In the event, Bernstein side-stepped responsibility for revealing this information, claiming with transparent insincerity that it had been beyond his editorial control.

Bernstein returned to *The Exception and the Rule* for the last two months of the year, but could not find a satisfactory lyricist with whom to work. The actor Zero Mostel had been engaged to appear, but the project never took wing, leaving its composer depressed. His feelings, like those of many creative artists, could range from elation to despair almost within moments of one another. At the end of the year, Bernstein flew to Rome to discuss a musical film about St Francis of Assisi with Franco Zeffirelli but would not commit himself further than this discussion stage.

His final months with the New York Philharmonic displayed the wide range of Bernstein's conducting talent, whatever he may have thought of some of the music he conducted. In January, they performed the extremely complex *Relata II* by Milton Babbitt and, as the season drew to a close, Bruckner's Ninth Symphony, Verdi's Requiem, Beethoven's *Missa solemnis* and scenes from Wagner's *Tristan und Isolde*.

In April of 1969, Sam Bernstein died, aged seventy-seven. In their final years together, Bernstein's parents had found a deep understanding and affection far removed from the coldness and bickering of their youth. Samuel and Leonard also achieved a mutual respect and love that compensated for their years of alienation. The funeral service took place at Temple Mishkan Tefila, which had moved from the old building in Roxbury to the suburb of Newton. Bernstein later rescheduled his programmes at the Philharmonic to include his *Jeremiah* Symphony, dedicated to his father.

It was a time of farewells. With the death of Sam Bernstein, all Leonard's 'father figures' – Mitropoulos, Koussevitzky, Reiner – had departed, and it was also time to say goodbye to the New York Philharmonic which, despite its demands, had sustained and supported him for more than a decade. He had first appeared with the orchestra more than a quarter of a century earlier. His final concert as Music Director was a moving performance of Mahler's great Third Symphony in D minor, the work that he had conducted as a memorial to Mitropoulos. It was, of course, received with a standing

Bernstein rehearses the New
York Philharmonic for the last
time as its Music Director,
15 May 1969.

ovation, during which Bernstein spent a long moment facing the orchestra, his back to the cheering audience, for once unable to find words adequate for the moment. Among the many praise-filled reviews was one from Harold Schonberg, who had been Bernstein's conscience as much as his enemy for such a long period of his tenure (and whose final complaint had been that the conductor had chosen the wrong moment to leave the orchestra).

The management of the New York Philharmonic had given him a speedboat called *Laureate* as a farewell present, but Bernstein was probably more touched by the gift that the members of the orchestra chose: a handmade silver and gold *mezuzah*, a small box containing religious texts which Jews fix to the doorposts of their homes. He would, of course, return to the New York Philharmonic many times as a guest conductor, but a golden era, in his own life as much as that of the orchestra, had come to an end.

For twelve years, Bernstein had concentrated his attention on conducting, and on taming and restoring the New York Philharmonic to a premier position among American orchestras. In addition, he had successfully developed a new form of educational entertainment on television. In the final years of his New York association, he had broadened his activities to create stronger and more important European links, further establishing himself as an international artist. They had been action-packed years and although two major works – *Kaddish* and *Chichester Psalms* – came from that period, composing had been forced to take a secondary role. The greatest challenge he would face in the next decade would be to find a balance between his appearances on the concert podium and his never-ending struggle to create the classical masterpiece by which he hoped to be remembered.

4

Bernstein in 1970 at a press
conference in the Royal
Festival Hall, London, before
recording Verdi's Requiem in
the Royal Albert Hall

*The work I have been writing all my life is
about the struggle that is born of the crisis of
our century, a crisis of faith.*

Leonard Bernstein,
at a press conference in 1977

Frustrations and Successes 1969–79

Bernstein first announced that he would be leaving the New York Philharmonic in the autumn of 1966, long before his actual departure date. If he really had intended to 'concentrate maximally on composing', he would have had time enough to free his engagement calendar of all future conducting commitments. In fact, while release from the Philharmonic gave him greater time for composing, he used much of his new 'freedom' to establish stronger conducting relationships with various European orchestras, most notably the Vienna Philharmonic. To assist him in achieving this, he had the services of Amberson Productions.

Amberson Productions, dating from 1969, was an extension of Bernstein's music publishing company, Amberson Enterprises, which had been formed a decade earlier to look after all his publishing interests in both classical and Broadway material. The new company, headed by Executive Producer Schuyler Chapin (whom Bernstein had known from Columbia Records since 1959), was set up for the creation of videotapes and films of Bernstein performances. Chapin's task was to establish co-production deals with partners in the video world who would provide the technical facilities and distribution. The first of these was London Weekend Television who, early in 1970, made a spectacular film of Verdi's Requiem in St Paul's Cathedral. Chapin later set up a valuable agreement with Unitel Productions in Munich, who undertook to film Bernstein conducting all of Mahler's symphonies, as well as various documentaries.

In 1971 Chapin would leave Amberson to become Deputy Manager of the Metropolitan Opera, to be succeeded by Harry Kraut, another Boston friend and Harvard graduate, who had served for some years with the Boston Symphony, notably at Tanglewood. Equally as courteous as the patrician Chapin, Kraut's soft-spoken manner belied a razor-sharp mind that helped to establish Amberson as an international business operation, whose activities would include film and television co-productions, publishing and even a change of record companies. His title eventually became Executive Vice-President, his principal function being to develop long-term plans, dividing periods of time between conducting and composing according to Bernstein's instructions. Bernstein had now set up a management organization dedicated to his needs, which would look after all his business interests and leave him free to concentrate entirely on musical matters: composing, conducting, filming, recording or whatever else might arise.

Within forty-eight hours of saying farewell to the New York musicians, Bernstein flew to Vienna to conduct Beethoven's *Missa solemnis*, marking the centenary of the Vienna State Opera. After three triumphant performances, where he was again fêted by presidents and chancellors, he joined Franco Zeffirelli in Rome to work again on the film about St Francis. Later in the summer of 1969, he invited the songwriter Paul Simon (originally of the Simon and Garfunkel partnership) to contribute to the film. Nothing came of it in the end, and Zeffirelli went on to make *Brother Sun, Sister Moon*, using music by the folk singer-songwriter Donovan. Even as Bernstein's interest in the Zeffirelli film was waning, he was seduced by another plan, this time suggested by the Israeli actor Topol: a musical version of Bertold Brecht's *The Caucasian Chalk Circle*. Bernstein set to work, but that project did not see completion either.

His 'maximal' composing plans had to be set aside yet again by January of 1970. He had agreed to conduct the New York Philharmonic in a concert performance of Beethoven's *Fidelio*, to mark the two-hundredth anniversary of Beethoven's birth. The Juilliard School of Music had just moved to its new home in Lincoln Center, and Bernstein (who had also committed himself to conducting a new production of *Fidelio* later in the year in Vienna) decided to use Juilliard students for the New York presentation.

In the midst of their preparations, he received an anguished call for help from Franco Zeffirelli. The Metropolitan Opera's traditional double-bill of Mascagni's *Cavalleria rusticana* and Leoncavallo's *I pagliacci* had been postponed because of an extended strike at the opera house. The rescheduling had been for January, but the original conductor and cast were no longer available. Bernstein agreed to conduct *Cavalleria*, sharing the podium with Fausto Cleva, but added a somewhat implausible argument for reversing the traditional order –

it is always 'Cav-and-Pag' – of the works. Schuyler Chapin, representing Bernstein's Amberson Productions, found an unsympathetic
Intendant at the 'Met' in Rudolf Bing who, suspecting that Bernstein
simply wanted to top the bill by taking the second half of the evening,
was unwilling to change the order of the operas, particularly as the set
change would extend the interval too far into the evening.

Bernstein plunged into two-fold rehearsals – *Fidelio* in the
mornings and *Cavalleria rusticana* in the afternoons – with his usual
zest. Sad to say, neither production fared well. Bernstein's tempos in
the Mascagni were so dozy that even his loyal friend Zeffirelli later
admitted that they were self-indulgent, and he was criticized the
following week for using Juilliard students in an opera as demanding
as *Fidelio*. All in all, his return conducting appearances in New York
enjoyed little acclaim.

Between October of the preceding year and January of 1970,
Bernstein found himself at the centre of two controversial issues
concerning civil rights and his own attitudes towards members of
America's black population. Anyone who knew Bernstein was aware of
his liberal policies, his left-wing sympathies and his constant and often
vocal opposition to any form of right-wing establishment. He had
opposed Eisenhower and Nixon to the point that Senator McCarthy's
investigators and Hoover's FBI minions had kept a close watch on
him, and it was suggested that he had even lost some of the valuable
patronage of his friend Jack Kennedy because of his continued
opposition to America's involvement in Vietnam.

It was therefore with some astonishment that he learned that the
City Commission on Human Rights decided that the New York
Philharmonic had discriminated against black musicians in its
employment policies during his tenure as Music Director. Two black
musicians, Earl Madison and Arthur Davis, who had failed to gain
appointments during auditions, claimed that they had not been
appointed because of their colour. (They had suggested a 'blindfold'
test, playing behind screens, but Bernstein had always favoured a
policy whereby players should be seen as well as heard, displaying
technique as well as musical skills.) In his testimony, Bernstein, who
had visibly supported the work of black musicians throughout his
career (including the appointment of the violinist Sanford Allen to the
Philharmonic in 1962, and of an assistant conductor, James de Priest,

in 1965), expressed the opinion that not enough black student musicians (i.e., musicians cultivating their studies by working with professional groups) were given adequate preparation for an orchestral career. If certain black musicians had auditioned for places in the orchestra and had not been chosen, it was simply because they did not display the necessary skills. The two musicians who claimed discrimination lost their case and, although the Commission accepted the Philharmonic's audition system, it suggested that there was bias in the orchestra's method of selecting substitute players when they were required.

For his part Bernstein was exonerated, but, during this period of acute social awareness of past evils, his image could still be tarnished in a form of guilt by association. (At this time personnel departments trembled at the thought of having to dismiss any black employee, even for the most justifiable reason, for fear of being accused of infringing civil rights.)

The second case was more embarrassing. Felicia Bernstein, in addition to her support of pacifists like Senator Eugene McCarthy, had involved herself in many causes where civil rights were under fire. One of the cases that had come to her attention involved twenty-one members of the Black Panther movement, who had been held in detention for nine months awaiting trial. The Black Panthers were a notorious and potentially dangerous revolutionary group and the

Under the Black Panther banner, members of the organization raise their fists in salute at the funeral in California of George Jackson, a prisoner in San Quentin who died during an abortive escape attempt.

charges against them were serious, including plans to kill policemen, bomb police stations, and to attack shops and railway stations. They were being held on bail so high, however, that none of them could raise it, with the result that they were being kept in solitary confinement, without funds even to pay for their defence. Their wives and children were also unsupported and suffering.

Understandably, Felicia was outraged that the law was being manipulated in such a way that the Black Panthers had been held prisoner for the best part of a year without a fair hearing. She organized an elegant reception at the Bernstein home on Park Avenue. After drinks and canapés for one hundred guests, including well-known figures from the entertainment world and leaders of the black community, as well as several important representatives of the Black Panthers, an invitation was made to hear speeches and to contribute to a fund for the defendants and their families.

It was a well-intentioned gesture, but it misfired disastrously. Whatever ill treatment the twenty-one prisoners had been receiving, the Black Panthers were a self-declared anti-Semitic, military style organization which, while dedicated to defending the civil rights of Afro-Americans, also threatened urban guerrilla warfare and used slogans like 'Off (i.e., 'Kill') the Zionist imperialists!' Before opening her home to them, Felicia Bernstein should have done some background research. Even more importantly, she should have made sure that her husband, who could never resist taking centre stage at any public meeting, was not there.

With various members of the press present, including the brilliant writer and witty social observer Tom Wolfe, Bernstein engaged the Panthers' 'Field Marshal' Donald Cox in a public dialogue. Cox outlined Panther policies, using the familiar clichés of terrorist doctrine, which Bernstein acknowledged by using the black vernacular expression 'I dig absolutely'. (Later, he insisted that it was an impatient reply to Cox's question 'You dig?', but by then the damage had been done.) The *New York Times* reported the event and also relayed it overseas on its wire service, making Bernstein appear part-patronizing and entirely stupid for playing host to black urban terrorists.

Coming so soon after the Philharmonic hearings by the City Commission on Human Rights, it was very bad publicity and worse followed. He gave the first performance of *Fidelio* on the day the

report appeared, receiving a pronounced 'thumbs down' from Harold
Schonberg, together with a *Times* editorial denouncing the Bernstein
soirée as 'the sort of elegant slumming that degrades patrons and
patronized alike'. It mocked the memory of Martin Luther King Jr.
In addition, Jews across America and as far away as Israel were
confronted with the thought that the Bernsteins supported the Black
Panthers' anti-Semitism. His home was picketed, his family received
hate letters and he was booed at the Philharmonic. For Bernstein, who
loyally never blamed Felicia for arranging the evening, it was a
humiliating experience, and he completed a five-week season at the
Philharmonic to the accompaniment of cruel pot-shots in the press
and angry picketers at the concert hall.

Perhaps the unkindest report of all came from Tom Wolfe, writing
a superbly flamboyant and wickedly funny article called 'Radical Chic:
That Party at Lenny's' for *New York* magazine. Wolfe, whose colourful
language and imagery reads more like Dylan Thomas than journalism,
had already mentally coined the phrase 'radical chic' after witnessing
an elegant Long Island party on behalf of manual labourers. He saw
the whole Black Panther Affair as pure William Thackeray and had
considered using it in a book of essays on a contemporary *Vanity Fair*.
He lampoons Bernstein mercilessly, describing how 'Lenny treasures
"the art of conversation". He treasures it, monopolizes it,
conglomerates it ...' Bernstein is, according to Wolfe, 'the Great
Interrupter, the Village Explainer, the champion of Mental Jotto, the
Free Analyst, Mr. Let's Find Out ... until every human brain is
reduced finally to a clump of seaweed inside a burnt-out husk and
collapses, implodes, in one last crunch of terminal boredom.'

Humour, however cruel, can take the sting out of any situation,
and it is possible that Wolfe's savage caricature eventually softened the
blow to Bernstein's public image. It made New York's beloved 'Lenny'
look like a naïvely impetuous 'do-gooder' and egotistical attention-
seeker rather than the supporter of a dangerously anti-Semitic urban
terrorist group. It is also worth noting that, when the Panthers were
finally tried in 1971, the entire case collapsed and all the defendants
(whose families Felicia had only wanted to help) were set free.

By the time Wolfe's article appeared, Bernstein was in Vienna for
its Beethoven celebrations, including *Fidelio* at the State Opera, a
Beethoven birthday film and concerts with the Vienna Philharmonic.

He had travelled there via London, for the memorable video of Verdi's Requiem in St Paul's Cathedral; then to Paris; on to a production of *Fidelio* in Rome, and finally a performance of Beethoven's 'Eroica' in Israel. Hurtful as Wolfe's article was, Bernstein was surrounded by the rich, the powerful, the loyal and fawning, who could insulate him from the outside world. Herbert von Karajan, until then the undisputed musical supremo of Europe, brought the Berlin Philharmonic Orchestra to the Vienna festival, and it must have pleased Bernstein when Karl Löbl, Vienna's most influential music critic, favoured him over the magisterial Karajan.

By the summer, when Bernstein returned to Tanglewood as Artistic Adviser, his unwise participation in black politics was forgiven if not forgotten, and he quickly re-established his position as America's cultural leader in the encouragement and the enthusiasm he inspired in a new generation of musicians. His greeting speech, reported in the *New York Times*, cautioned against despair and 'dropping out' and offered active encouragement. 'We'll help you as much as we can – that's why we're here – but it is you who must produce it, with your new atomic minds, your flaming, angry hope, and your secret weapon of art.' From there, he took the New York Philharmonic to Japan, again accompanied by Seiji Ozawa.

Throughout this period Bernstein's creative powers had been focused, albeit with constant distractions, on his new work *Mass*. Using the Catholic service as the starting-point for a huge theatre piece, it was promised for the 1969 opening of the Kennedy Center in Washington (construction delays fortunately led to a rescheduled opening of the building in the summer of 1971). Late in 1970 much of the score was written – either new material or music salvaged from other projects – but it had neither a director nor a lyricist. By February of 1971, however, he was back 'on the road' again: to Paris, then touring with the Vienna Philharmonic, giving twelve concerts in fifteen days. During a two-week break from their travels, he again performed and recorded *Der Rosenkavalier* in Vienna with a team from Decca Records, led by John Culshaw, who had been lent to CBS for the project. From there, he travelled to Israel for additional concerts. The schedule was as exhausting as anything he had undertaken during his years with the New York Philharmonic. He returned to New York in early May, determined to concentrate on the completion of *Mass*, now scheduled to open in September. He was still searching for a satisfactory English text and lyrics for his music. Felicia, forever dedicated to civil rights causes, was currently organizing support for Father Philip Berrigan, a Catholic priest who, with several other peace workers, had been arrested for allegedly plotting to kidnap Henry Kissinger. Bernstein decided that such a churchman could offer suitable advice for a work dedicated to restoring faith in God during such troubled times. He visited Father Berrigan, who was being held in the Federal Correction Insitute in Danbury, Connecticut, but was unable to achieve much in the short meeting the prison authorities permitted. (The meeting prompted J. Edgar Hoover of the FBI to warn President Nixon that Bernstein's work, planned for the opening of the new Kennedy Center, might possibly contain a 'subversive' text.)

Bernstein was in a mood of deep depression when his sister Shirley, now an agent for writers, took him to see *Godspell*, by one of her clients, the 23-year-old Stephen Schwartz. Based on the Gospel according to Saint Matthew, the show was a religious rock musical in the genre epitomized by *Jesus Christ Superstar*, and was enjoying a highly successful New York run. Bernstein met Schwartz and was convinced that he had found the answer for his unfinished *Mass*. Superstitious as ever, he noted that the young writer, in addition to being a composer and lyricist, even had the same initials as Stephen Sondheim, who had brought such success to *West Side Story* (although many came to believe that initials were about the only attribute the two men had in common!).

Mass was completed very quickly by Bernstein and Schwartz, and a highly talented production team assembled. Gordon Davidson (who had successfully restaged *Candide* in Los Angeles) would direct, the brilliant Alvin Ailey, together with his dance ensemble, would be in charge of choreography, Oliver Smith would design the sets, and Maurice Peress would be musical director. Three more friends were invited to supervise the orchestration: Hershy Kay, Sid Ramin (to advise on the use of rock instruments) and Jonathan Tunick, who had recently worked on Stephen Sondheim's *Follies*.

Mass: A Theatre Piece for Singers, Players and Dancers, to give its full title, is Bernstein's most ambitious theatre work. Despite its adaptation of the Latin text, interspersed with songs, 'numbers', set-piece

Michael Hume as the
Celebrant in a televised
version of *Mass* for PBS's
'Theater in America' series,
27 February 1974

choreographic sequences (rather than formal ballets) and symphonic interludes, it is ecumenical in nature and does not fall into any exact category. Perhaps the closest description would be 'pageant', without its usual historical connotations. With a cast of two hundred, including dancers, singers, a boy chorus, rock singers, blues singers, actors and two orchestras – stage and pit – as well as a marching band that plays its way through the audience, it is a theatrical/musical 'experience'.

The story and its message are simple and self-explanatory. Following a Kyrie Eleison, pre-recorded quadrophonically (the ill-fated 'quad' system had only recently been introduced by the record industry), a young man dressed in shirt and jeans, with mandatory guitar, sings 'A Simple Song'. He becomes The Celebrant, suitably attired in priestly robes, but as he tries to celebrate the Mass, his 'congregation' turns against him with cynicism, anger and indifference, rejecting faith and, in the spirit of late 1960s/early 1970s youth, calling passionately for peace. At the most climactic moment of the 'service', the Celebrant smashes the sacramental vessels, throws off his priestly outer garments and, seemingly mad, rejects his congregation. Faith is reborn with the message that each of us must find our own way to restore peace to the world. The huge cast exchanges embraces and, as the choir of boys leaves the stage and passes through the theatre, they bring a 'touch of peace' to people sitting on aisle seats, exhorting the audience to 'pass it on'.

In the theatre, *Mass* is a powerful, sometimes intensely moving experience. Heard on records, the work contains some of Bernstein's most effective and deeply moving 'serious' music. Regrettably, much of the 'popular' music is uninspired and contains some lyrics that vary from the banal to the inane, with cliché-ridden imagery that would embarrass a back-room hack knocking out rock lyrics in the Brill Building (New York's 'Tin Pan Alley'). When Bernstein had played some of his 'pop' music intended for the Zeffirelli St Francis film to Paul Simon, the latter had been unimpressed. They tried working together, but nothing remains from their partnership except a stylish quatrain, which Simon donated to *Mass*. It is probably the best thing in the libretto:

Half of the people are stoned
And the other half are waiting for the next election.
Half the people are drowned
And the other half are swimming in the wrong direction.

The many popular musical styles Bernstein assembled into one work – including rock, blues, jazz, gospel and Broadway – sound dated and frankly 'corny' at times, even by 1971 standards. There are one or two moments of great charm, such as in the Sanctus and Agnus Dei, but even the Broadway side of these seems to hark back to *West Side Story*, written fifteen years earlier. When *Mass* opened at the Kennedy Center in Washington, a number of distinguished critics were highly impressed, including Paul Hume, who described Bernstein's music as the greatest he had written. Harold Schonberg, direct as ever, decided that it was a pseudo-serious effort at re-thinking the Mass that was basically 'cheap and vulgar', and suggested that Bernstein's problem was that he desperately wanted to be 'with it'.

Schonberg's comment was cruel, but contained more than a grain of harsh truth. There is no question of Bernstein's sincerity and his deeply felt desire for world peace, but the 51-year-old composer was simply not in touch with contemporary popular music. He was surely too well read, and had seen and heard too many skilled lyrics seriously to believe that the sloppy rhyming couplets and immature 'message' of the libretto were of the same standard, say, as Paul Simon's simple quatrain. But he deluded himself into believing that he was adopting a 'youthful' stance, possibly thinking that he could reach a younger audience with his message by talking to them in their own language. Even the inclusion of the latest audio 'gimmick' – quadraphonic sound – at various moments in the performance, was an ill-considered effort to be 'trendy'.

Nevertheless, the scope of his vision, the grand spectacle, some parts of the score (notably *Three Meditations*, later salvaged for the concert hall) and the intensity of the peace message made *Mass* an important – if flawed – theatrical experiment. Having been warned off, President Nixon did not attend the première, nor did Jacqueline Kennedy (although she went to the revival the following year and sent a note to Bernstein telling him that she loved it). Many members of the Kennedy clan (including the late President's eighty-year-old mother, Rose) were present, however, together with a host of leading political figures. The controversial 'sacrilege', the smashing of the sacramental vessels, caused a few ecclesiastical ripples, including a pastoral letter from an Archbishop in Cincinnati (who had not seen the work) forbidding Catholics to attend such a 'blasphemous' piece when it was peformed at a local festival in 1972.

New Yorkers saw *Mass* in 1972, when it again received mixed reviews but enjoyed a successful four-week run at the Metropolitan Opera with a 'cut down' cast of only one hundred and seventy-five(!). Yale University mounted an impressive production conducted by John Mauceri and, with Bernstein's approval, it was taken to the Konzerthaus in Vienna in 1973, where a consortium of European television companies made a video that was broadcast in many countries. There was a further production in Los Angeles in 1974, again directed by Gordon Davidson. To Bernstein's disappointment, wherever it was performed, it failed to achieve unanimous acceptance and, despite Aaron Copland's efforts on his behalf, it did not win the Pulitzer Prize for Music. Over the years, *Mass* has also been performed by college groups and many community theatres but, in post-*glasnost*, post-Vietnam, post-student rebellion times, it seems to represent a bygone era and its original passion has become diluted. It also recalls that period in the late 1960s and early 70s, when many middle-aged men (including, perhaps, Leonard Bernstein) suddenly adopted clothing styles more appropriate to youngsters half their age, imitated the jazz vernacular of teenagers, experimented with drugs, rediscovered politics and experienced the traumas of 'mid-life crisis'.

The summer of 1971 marked the change in the directorship of Amberson Productions from Schuyler Chapin to Harry Kraut. Chapin had done invaluable groundwork, but Kraut was to become the architect of an all-powerful international operation. Another newcomer to Amberson was Thomas Cothran, the music director of a local West Coast radio station, whom Bernstein had met (and with whom he had shared his bed) on a brief visit during the San Francisco run of *Candide*. He brought Cothran back to Washington during the final preparations for *Mass*, for which he proof-read the score.

Bernstein had rejected serialism and certain other experimental forms in his 1964–5 sabbatical year because such music (when composed by him) was not *honest*. With the possible exception of

Mass, designed to appeal to the popular culture of an era, he always remained faithful to his personal credo, maintaining his own unique and distinctively American voice. He was often criticized for swimming against a twelve-tone tide that had already gathered up Stravinsky and Copland (although it is questionable whether either composer wrote any serial works of lasting value). Bernstein also explained that, in his music, atonality represented anguish and uncertainty; tonality and accessibility were the foundations of faith and reassurance. Despite his need for a programme to trigger his imagination, Bernstein's creativity was instinctive rather than intellectual and he did not really need to explain or even rationalize it.

Opportunities to delve more deeply into his musical thought processes and, perhaps, to illustrate his personal philosophy of music presented themselves in the autumn of 1971, when he was invited to serve as the Charles Eliot Norton Professor of Poetry at Harvard University for 1972–3. This would involve his presence at the university for two terms, holding student seminars, as well as delivering six lectures. Such an invitation represented true academic recognition. Poets like T. S. Eliot, Robert Frost and W. H. Auden had delivered Norton lectures and Bernstein's musical predecessors included Copland, Hindemith and Stravinsky.

But before Bernstein could devote his attention to the Norton project, he had a full programme of concert commitments. Harry Kraut, building on well-established overseas connections, had arranged a new series of European concerts that included Stravinsky with the London Symphony Orchestra, preceded by an excellent Bernstein lecture projected on to a giant screen at the Royal Albert Hall, followed by Mahler concerts in Vienna. Bernstein's persuasive and powerful readings, which earned the highest critical praise, proved to players and public alike that Mahler's time had finally come. Unitel would film a complete Mahler cycle over the next few years. As part of that, Bernstein travelled from Vienna to Israel to film performances of *Das Lied von der Erde*.

In addition to a very heavy conducting schedule and assembling his thoughts for the Norton Lectures (for which Thomas Cothran had been brought in as a research assistant), Bernstein was working on two new composing projects. The first was a ballet, again suggested by Jerome Robbins (whose role as muse remained constant throughout

Bernstein in full flight during a performance of Mahler's 'Resurrection' Symphony at Tanglewood in July of 1970. The conductor received an eleven-minute ovation.

Bernstein's creative life), based on the Yiddish folk tale *The Dybbuk*. The work would be presented as part of the celebrations in the spring of 1973 for the twenty-fifth anniversary of the founding of the state of Israel. The second was a new musical for Broadway, although it is unlikely that Bernstein, at that point, considered his projects in old-fashioned 'Broadway musical' terms. With *West Side Story* and, even more, *Mass*, he had carried the concept of American music-theatre beyond the clichés of the Broadway show. Just as the Eisenhower administration and the activities of the House Un-American Activities Committee had spurred the creation of *Candide*, so the ominous presence of Richard Nixon and his seemingly inexorable takeover of the White House led Alan Jay Lerner to approach Bernstein with the idea of creating a new musical, based on the history of that Presidential residence which, for many, represented America itself. Lerner was an old friend and fellow Harvard alumnus from the same era, and had already become a theatrical 'legend' through his partnership with Frederick Loewe. Their shows together had included *Brigadoon*, *My Fair Lady*, *Camelot*, and the film *Gigi*, and his career had faltered following Loewe's retirement. This new partnership, of the most successful lyricist in the theatre with its most brilliant composer, must have seemed, therefore, to be an unbeatable combination.

There was a touch of Thornton Wilder (*The Long Christmas Dinner*, *The Skin of our Teeth*) in the concept of the plot, in which the same cast acted several generations of Presidents and First Ladies and their black servants in a play about the various tenants of *1600 Pennsylvania Avenue*, the most famous address in Washington and, for that matter, the United States of America. There was also a nod in the direction of Marc Blitzstein and his European forerunners in the play's format, which would reveal a rehearsal in which members of the cast would discuss the historical context of their roles. All in all, it was an ambitious and challenging project that would require all of Lerner's and Bernstein's skills to bring off successfully.

In the autumn of 1972, before he could concentrate his attention on any of his creative projects, Bernstein had committed himself to further public performances. Gören Gentele, newly appointed as general manager of the Metropolitan Opera in place of Rudolf Bing, had persuaded him to open the company's season with a new

Bernstein in London on his way to conduct a Stravinsky memorial at the Royal Albert Hall, 4 April 1972

production of Bizet's *Carmen*. The offer was irresistible to Bernstein, who had loved the opera since childhood days. But at Tanglewood that summer, Bernstein learned of Gentele's tragic death in a holiday car accident. Schuyler Chapin became acting general manager at the Met in his place, and Bernstein agreed to continue with the production.

Although it would be expensive, the occasion seemed an ideal opportunity to record the opera. A classical recording of this size in America was extremely expensive and CBS was unwilling to make the investment. Goddard Lieberson, the brilliant and articulate classically-trained President of CBS, and a firm believer that profits from the popular side should subsidize classical operations, had retired. His replacement, Clive Davis, was intent on developing the company's contemporary image and, while he did not stifle classical efforts, took the 'bottom line' approach that they should be self-supporting. The company was, furthermore, in the midst of some acrimonious accounting disputes with Harry Kraut, who had discovered serious discrepancies dating back anything up to fifteen years.

Waiting in the wings, the prestigious Deutsche Grammophon GmbH of Hamburg (DGG), the classical market leader in most countries, was having difficulties in matching CBS and RCA in the all-important American market; they were therefore happy to take on the recording. In addition, the classically dedicated DGG, whose strong European associations included the Vienna and Berlin Philharmonic Orchestras, would be an increasingly important ally for possible future Bernstein collaborations.

Carmen opened at the Met in September of 1972 to excellent reviews, and Bernstein brought his exclusive CBS association to an end by recording the production for DGG, thus earning the new company excellent worldwide sales. His time with CBS had been mutually profitable for many years, but by the time Bernstein signed a new and exclusive agreement with DGG a few years later, CBS had come to take Bernstein somewhat for granted. Amberson, for example, had been expected to contribute to the cost of recording *Mass* (it would turn out to be a classical bestseller). CBS, which had become the most successful 'pop' music organization in the world, was, quite frankly, losing interest in all classical recordings. Bernstein's new association with DGG would result in re-recording a large part of his repertoire, including nearly all his own music, mostly in Vienna, Israel and London.

In the autumn of 1972, Bernstein set up residence at Harvard to begin his year as Eliot Norton Professor. For him it was an idyllic return to the golden years of his youth. He loved to be with young people, he was a born teacher and, even more gratifying, he could hold centre stage at all times because it was required of him! The six Norton Lectures, not yet written, were to be accompanied on screens by well-illustrated (and expensive) pre-shot films giving musical examples. Working in the background, Harry Kraut devised a well-planned commercial campaign, calling for a second, televised studio presentation of the lectures, which would then be made available in book form, on discs and on video-cassettes. Funding was not available, and Amberson footed the bill. In the meantime, Bernstein attended various social functions, gave seminars, made the acquaintance of many students and endeared himself to the academic community, to the point of being named 'Man of the Year' by the university magazine. But the lectures were still incomplete and, because of further public commitments in early 1973, Bernstein eventually obtained permission to delay them to the autumn (and next semester) of the year.

Bernstein had never lost sight of the disastrous continuing situation in Vietnam and, in January of 1973, he travelled to Washington to give a concert called 'A Plea for Peace' at the National Cathedral. Here he conducted Haydn's *Mass in Time of War* on the same evening that the newly sworn-in Nixon was being entertained at his inaugural concert at the Kennedy Center. The Bernstein performance, before an audience of three thousand with a further twelve thousand outside, listening to the music over loudspeakers, completely overshadowed the Nixon celebrations, and was hailed both nationally and internationally.

After a brief holiday in the Canary Islands with his friends Christoph Eschenbach and Justus Frantz, Bernstein returned to Harvard to complete work on the Norton Lectures. His many years of television experience were invaluable in the preparation of the complicated and sophisticated material that would be displayed during the course of each lecture. This was perhaps the key to one of the problems of the Norton talks. Throughout his television career,

whether in the 'Omnibus' programmes or the Young People's
Concerts, Bernstein had always displayed a special skill for making the
unfamiliar accessible and the difficult comprehensible. The Norton
Lectures would deal with an abstract theory and, in its application to
music, it would become almost unfathomable to all but the most
carefully honed musical minds, even though the overriding message
Bernstein wanted to convey could probably have been expressed in
one or two simple sentences.

Before the finished presentations could be 'put to bed', ready for
the autumn, there were to be further interruptions to his schedule.
The first was an invitation from Pope Paul VI to conduct a concert at
the Vatican, where Bernstein would perform Bach's Magnificat and his
own *Chichester Psalms*. The concert in the Vatican's huge auditorium
was a triumphant success for Bernstein, the more so given the
rejection of *Mass* by various Catholic organizations in the United
States. It was televised and shown across Europe. Shortly after this,
Bernstein travelled to Vienna to see the Yale production of *Mass* in
Vienna, which was also televised. He missed Tanglewood, pleading
the need to continue on the Norton Lectures (also to work on the
ballet *Dybbuk*), but returned to Israel for filmed concerts, to London
for a television production of *Trouble in Tahiti*, to the Edinburgh
Festival for Mahler with the London Symphony Orchestra, and
thence to Ely Cathedral for a Unitel film of Mahler's 'Resurrection'
Symphony. Between these engagements, he managed to squeeze in
further visits to his friends in the Canary Islands. It was a typical
Bernstein period in that he was constantly on the move.

The first of the Eliot Norton lectures was given on 9 October 1973.
As an overall title for the series, Bernstein chose *The Unanswered
Question*, borrowed from an enigmatic 1906 work by the eccentric
American composer Charles Ives. The Ives piece features an off-stage
string choir ('The Silences of the Druids') which establishes a calm
mood, against which the onstage wind instruments, notably the
trumpet, ask a discordant 'Perennial Question of Existence', searching
in vain for the 'Invisible Answer'. Most observers, however, assume
that Bernstein used the title in order to pose the question 'Whither
music?'. Bernstein himself stated that he was no longer sure what the
question was, except that the answer was 'Yes'. It is more likely that, as

with Ravel's *Pavane pour une Infante défunte*, he just 'liked the sound of the words'!

The basic and simple message of Bernstein's lectures was that music must be – like any natural phenomenon – perceived and understood instinctively. In other words, he was defending tonal music against the artificiality and the mathematical calculations of Arnold Schoenberg's blind alley of serialism, in which the natural instincts of all musicians had been enslaved by a theoretical system of music-making that had no rationale but its own creation.

The composer and teacher Arnold Schoenberg (1874–1951) is generally regarded as the father of serialism, or twelve-tone music, and founder of the Second Viennese School, whose many adherents included Alban Berg and Anton Webern and, in later years, Pierre Boulez and Milton Babbitt. Perhaps the most famous twentieth-century composers to adopt serial techniques in their later years were Igor Stravinsky and Aaron Copland. Shortly after World War I, Schoenberg's many years of experimenting with music that no longer had a tonal framework, together with what he described as 'the desire for a conscious control of the new means and forms', led him to compose arranging the twelve notes of the chromatic scale in a particular order, which he called a 'tone row'. The series of notes is always used complete, without note repetition before finishing the 'row', although the composer may choose the initial order in which the notes are used, their length, and many other permutations and combinations.

For Bernstein, the language of the Second Viennese School was artificial, both in its conception and in its illustrations, whereas melody (in a tonal framework) was as natural as spoken language is a form of human communication. To demonstrate this, he drew an analogy with the work of the linguist Noam Chomsky, who argues that all human languages have a single common origin. The same principle, Bernstein claimed, can be applied to music; he aimed to show to his audience, sometimes with speculation, sometimes with absolute truths, that tonality is a natural law, part of the human condition, and that all music has emerged from the same, universally common elements.

The lectures were brilliant, articulate and, at times, densely concentrated. The first three discussed musical phonology, syntax and

A CBS birthday party for Bernstein at the Edinburgh Festival in 1973. Seated on the couch are Felicia Bernstein, Leonard Bernstein, Pierre Boulez, Daniel Barenboim and Jacqueline du Pré.

grammar (again drawing linguistic parallels), while the second three, 'The Delights and Danger of Ambiguity' (Berlioz to Wagner to Debussy), 'The Twentieth-Century Crisis' (Ravel, Schoenberg and Mahler) and 'The Poetry of the Earth' (Stravinsky), examined the various courses that musical language has followed.

Not unexpectedly, response to his arguments was divided down the middle, especially as many of his theories were based on speculation rather than hard fact. Even Bernstein's critics had to agree that his proposals were stimulating and often daring, and that his own love of and dedication to music shone through every sentence. It is interesting to note, however, that some of his severest critics attacked the Eliot Norton Lectures not at an intellectual level but more often as a personal criticism of the man delivering the message. Michael Steinberg, a Boston critic, wrote in the *New York Times* of Bernstein's 'fatal gift of projecting himself rather than the topic at hand'.

The end of the year saw an important revival of *Candide*, directed by Harold Prince, with a new book by Hugh Wheeler and additional lyrics by Stephen Sondheim. It first played at the Chelsea Theater Center in Brooklyn before transferring to the Broadway Theatre in Manhattan, which had been specially reconstructed to accommodate a set that extended into the auditorium. Bernstein put on a brave face, but was clearly unhappy with the highly truncated version; even so, it proved to be the most successful version thus far in its patchwork history, and played for nearly two years. It was difficult to argue with such success.

With the Norton Lectures behind him, Bernstein was finally able to concentrate on composing. *Dybbuk*, originally intended for Israel's twenty-fifth birthday celebrations, was already a year late, but work on the ballet progressed slowly in the first part of 1974. Although the story has folk origins, Bernstein and Robbins chose the Yiddish drama of the same name by Shlomo Ansky. A *dybbuk* is the spirit that seeks to enter the body of a living person and Ansky's play has a familiar folk plot. Two young men swear an oath of friendship, stating that if one has a son and the other a daughter, their children will be joined in marriage. The friends separate and, as fate would have it, their offspring – a son, Channon, and a daughter, Leah – meet and fall in love. When the story begins, however, one of the fathers has died; the other has forgotten his pledge and has arranged

Bernstein photographed
conducting in the late 1970s

for Leah to be married to a wealthy suitor. Desperate, Channon calls
upon the powers of the forbidden *Kabbalah*. Using black magic
words that evoke satanic forces, he is destroyed by them in a moment
of fierce ecstasy. At Leah's wedding, his spirit returns as a *dybbuk* and
enters her. She becomes a person possessed, now speaking with
Channon's voice. A court is held to exorcize the *dybbuk*, but
Channon will not release Leah from her father's pledge. The curse of
God (anathema) is declared and the *dybbuk* is expelled, but Leah
cannot exist without her predestined bridegroom, and gives up her
life to join him in oblivion.

Dybbuk was first performed by the New York City Ballet in May 1974, and received excellent reviews, both for the music and the choreography. Yet it did not inspire great public enthusiasm. Jerome Robbins was one of the finest choreographers of his generation, and yet he is usually most remembered for his light-hearted and humorous creations, like *Fanfare* (using Britten's *Young Person's Guide to the Orchestra*), *The Recital* (Chopin) or, indeed, *Fancy Free*. He had worked slowly on *Dybbuk* – for once, Bernstein was not to blame for all the delays! – but was still unsatisfied with it, making further modifications in later seasons. In 1980, he choreographed an entirely new ballet, *Suite of Dances*, using the same music. By the early 1990s, both ballets had been taken from the City Ballet's programmes, suffering a similar fate to that of *Facsimile*, the second ballet collaboration with Bernstein from 1946, which was respectfully received, but dropped from the repertoire of the Ballet Theatre within five years.

Fortunately, Bernstein salvaged most of *Dybbuk*'s score, which is one of his best, in two orchestral suites, performed in separate concerts the following year. His final Eliot Norton lecture, entitled 'The Poetry of the Earth' and using *Oedipus Rex* as its mainstay, had been devoted to the music of Stravinsky, and there is little doubt that the great Russian composer is the guiding influence of the first half (and first suite) of *Dybbuk*. While Stravinsky's music is inspired either by the Russian Orthodox church or the all-powerful national musical traditions of his motherland, Bernstein's music, to use Jack Gottlieb's description, is 'deeply rooted in the soil of Eastern European folklore'. One could also substitute 'Jewish' for 'European'; parts of the score echo the Russian Jewish tradition, which Bernstein had absorbed through his father. He described the first suite as 'the music of this world' with 'a Jewish sound', which he amplified by the use of two cantor-like singers, performing excerpts from the liturgy and quoting from The Book of Samuel and The Song of Solomon.

The second suite, taken from that part of the ballet dealing with the rituals of the *Kabbalah* and the ceremony of exorcism, is wrapped up in mysterious compositional methods involving numerology and anagrams. Bernstein was particularly fascinated by the dualities expressed throughout Ansky's original drama: good and evil, ends and means, male and female, self and society, etc. Despite his dislike of

serial composition, he developed a sort of personal 'system' to create
the abstract effects for 'the music of the True World' and its duality
with 'the music of this world'. As with all Bernstein's 'programmes'
and extended explanations, however, they should be treated only as an
interesting side aspect of the music. Both suites of *Dybbuk*, while they
may be very different from one another, can be enjoyed without any
specific foreknowledge of their contexts.

Bernstein returned to Tanglewood in the summer of 1974. There
had been domestic health crises in the preceding months. Felicia had
required a mastectomy to remove a malignant growth, a forewarning
perhaps of the cancer that was to take her life within five years. The
operation did not persuade her to give up smoking. A few weeks later,
Leonard had also been under observation in hospital, following the
discovery of ectopic beats in his heart rhythm. Despite exaggerated
news reports, no serious damage was revealed and he, too, remained a
dedicated three-pack-a-day smoker.

With the launching of *Dybbuk*, Bernstein was ready to concentrate
on *1600 Pennsylvania Avenue* but, once again, public appearances
around the world took precedence. First there was a New York
Philharmonic tour of Japan, shared with Boulez, the orchestra's new
musical director, followed almost immediately by concerts in Vienna
and a brief stopover in England. He worked with Lerner in the latter
part of the year, but there were continuing 'book' problems. After a
holiday in the Caribbean, he met again with Lerner, who had resisted
'help' from various possible directors. Occasionally, concert
engagements interrupted their efforts, but Bernstein dedicated himself
to the task throughout the first part of 1975. By the summer, it was
still incomplete.

Europe's major musical celebration took place in Salzburg every
summer, where the proceedings were always dominated by Herbert
von Karajan. Bernstein, however, who had previously enjoyed only a
brief visit with the New York Philharmonic, now made a triumphant
return to the festival with two appearances: the first with the London
Symphony Orchestra, and the second with the Vienna Philharmonic.
In the background, his new-found friends at DGG offered powerful,
if discreet, support (Karajan was also under contract to DGG). Not to
be outdone, the European marketing forces of CBS who, at that
point, had over two hundred Bernstein records in their catalogue,

used the opportunity to fill every advertising space with Bernstein portraits and posters advertising Bernstein's CBS recordings. The temperature of the cool 'cordial' relations between the conductors dropped steadily by the minute and, to the delight of a few insiders, the two giants of the podium spent much of their time upstaging one another. If it was a contest, Bernstein probably emerged the winner, with an inspired performance of Mahler's huge Eighth Symphony that was the highlight of the whole festival.

From Salzburg, the Bernstein circus travelled to Edinburgh, appearing with both the London Symphony Orchestra and the Orchestre Nationale (the French radio orchestra). From there, he moved to Paris for a spectacular television and record undertaking: the massive Berlioz Requiem ('Grande Messe des morts'), whose huge choral and orchestral forces include four off-stage brass ensembles, placed high up in galleries in the four corners of the building. It was performed in Les Invalides (the church of Saint-Louis-des-Invalides) which houses Napoleon's tomb and is the site for which Berlioz had originally conceived the work. It was the major social and musical event of the year, attended by President Giscard d'Estaing.

Bernstein could not return to *1600 Pennsylvania Avenue* until late September, when he found the show on the brink of collapse. The producer Arnold Saint-Subber had quit, to be replaced by the ever-loyal Roger Stevens (who had originally come to the rescue of *West Side Story*). Stevens wanted reassurance that the troublesome book was resolved before he started to raise funds for the production, but Lerner side-stepped the problem by contacting an old friend, J. Paul Austin, an executive of Coca-Cola, who backed the show with an initial payment of $900,000. A show about the White House was an ideal vehicle for the bicentennial year, less than three months away, and Coca-Cola were satisfied that the names of Lerner and Bernstein were guarantee enough of its success.

They were wrong. Lerner's book, and possibly some of Bernstein's music, needed a great deal of work, but the bicentennial year was upon them and the producers were dazzled by Coca-Cola's support. Rehearsals began late in January of 1976, directed by Frank Corsaro, who had worked both on Broadway and in the opera house. Although lengthy, the Bernstein score seemed to work well enough, but Lerner's weighty book cried out for revisions that he was not prepared to make. The show opened in Philadelphia in late February and, following an apologetic curtain-speech by Bernstein, ran for nearly four hours. Bernstein's music was applauded, but Lerner's words received the brunt of an almost unanimously hostile press. In addition, the Lerner–Bernstein birthday tribute to the nation became, because of the earnestness of its 'message', a bitter criticism of some of the early residents of the White House.

Various friends were invited to Philadelphia to see whether the ailing show could be 'doctored', including Jerome Robbins, Arthur Laurents and Mike Nichols, but they all came away with the conclusion that it was beyond repair and recommended closing it without further embarrassment. Lerner refused, adding that Coca-Cola's funding was also predicated on a Broadway opening. Ten days before the show moved to Washington for further try-outs, Corsaro (who had loyally remained with the production for eight months) departed, accompanied by his choreographer Donald McKayle. They were replaced by Gilbert Moses and George Faison, two black directors who had worked on the musical *The Wiz*, a black version of *The Wizard of Oz*, which had enjoyed a very successful Broadway run. It was suggested that they might have fewer problems with cutting down the endless references to racial injustice that seemed to drag the show to a standstill. They did make some cuts but chose to retain certain scenes that depicted black servants in the White House as wide-eyed innocents. This was a little too close to the character of Rochester in Jack Benny's comedy shows of the 1940s and 50s, and the show later found itself described by *Time* magazine as 'racist'.

After unsuccessful attempts to restore some life during the Washington run, *1600 Pennsylvania Avenue* opened in New York on 4 May 1976, but closed after only seven performances. Disastrous reviews served as its epitaph and Bernstein forbade any original cast recording.

There is little question that the book was the major cause of the catastrophe, but it may be that Lerner, whose previous successes with Loewe had been in the tradition of the Viennese operetta, would never have blended cohesively with Bernstein, whose *Mass* had already carried him far beyond the confines of a 'traditional' musical show. The basic problem, according to some, was that Lerner set out to write a musical and Bernstein to compose an opera. As ever with

MARK HELLINGER THEATRE

ROGER L. STEVENS and ROBERT WHITEHEAD

present

KEN HOWARD	PATRICIA ROUTLEDGE	GILBERT PRICE

in

1600 PENNSYLVANIA AVENUE

A Musical About the Problems of Housekeeping

Book and Lyrics by   *Music by*

ALAN JAY LERNER   LEONARD BERNSTEIN

with

EMILY YANCY

EDWIN STEFFE   JOHN WITHAM   RALPH FARNWORTH   HECTOR JAIME MERCADO
CARL HALL   HOWARD ROSS   DAVID E. THOMAS   ALEXANDER ORFALY   GUY COSTLEY
and **REID SHELTON**

Scenery Designed by   *Lighting by*
KERT LUNDELL   **THARON MUSSER**

Costumes Coordinated by
WHITNEY BLAUSEN & DONA GRANATA

Musical Director   *Orchestrations by*   *Sound Design by*
ROLAND GAGNON   SID RAMIN and HERSHY KAY   JOHN McCLURE
Hair Stylist **WERNER SHERER**

Entire Production Co-Directed, Staged and Choreographed by
GILBERT MOSES and GEORGE FAISON

Produced by arrangement with **SAINT SUBBER**

Leonard Bernstein, there were some excellent musical contributions. One of his songs, 'Take Care of This House', has been adopted as an inaugural anthem. It was sung by Frederica von Stade at Jimmy Carter's Presidential Inauguration Gala in 1977. A production number called 'Rehearse', originally conceived for the opening of the show, was later adapted and used in *Slava!*, a tribute to the Russian cellist and conductor, Mstislav Rostropovich.

Opposite, the New York programme for the ill-fated Lerner–Bernstein collaboration, which lasted for only seven performances

Throughout Bernstein's marriage, there is no question that he remained constant in his love for Felicia and in his devotion to his family. She, in return, loved and supported him to the point of abandoning her own successful stage and television career. She also maintained a gently restraining hand on his excesses, whether helping him choose his wardrobe and look after his appearance (she cut and styled his hair for many years), or persuading him not to buy ostentatious cars and other unnecessary success symbols. Quiet, always elegant, refined and dignified, she provided the stability that her husband, forever living on the edge of professional and emotional exaggeration, needed.

However devoted he was, Bernstein could never escape his homosexual impulses, and it is difficult to assess how soon after their marriage he strayed into casual masculine sexual encounters. For the most part, they had little significance beyond quick physical and emotional gratification for a man with oversize appetites, although some of these attachments extended over longer periods of time. He was a bisexual man with strong feelings for traditional family ties, and Felicia, while she did not necessarily discuss his extra-marital infidelities, was certainly aware of them. Perhaps she thought that marriage would eventually change him, or even that maturity, age and a consequent reduction of sexual drive would lay his 'demon' to rest. In the early years of their marriage, her letters sometimes exhorted him not to be too 'pervy' when he was in Rome in the company of well-known homosexuals but, over the years, their correspondence is generally filled with an intimate love and deep affection that would have been impossible to maintain if it had not been genuine.

Bernstein's less friendly biographers cite times when Felicia was humiliated by his constant flirting with men (even in her *macho* native Chile, when he was there on tour with the New York Philharmonic) or absenting himself with men at parties they were both attending, to

The Bernsteins, at Heathrow airport, prepare for colder climes.

return looking tousled and dishevelled. The stories contain an element of truth combined with *schadenfreude* but, for the most part, Bernstein – who was a constant and dedicated exhibitionist – showed appropriate discretion.

On a number of occasions he did treat Felicia poorly, by subjecting her to cheap jibes, but being a vain man, constantly in the spotlight of attention, he may not have been fully aware of any hurt he might be inflicting. There is the much cited example of the rehearsal of Honegger's *Jeanne d'Arc au Bûcher*, in the late 1950s, when Felicia's lines read 'What is that dog howling in the night?' and Bernstein quipped, 'That's no dog; that's my wife!' His critics immediately seized upon it, claiming that Felicia was wounded by him. They overlooked the fact, however, that he was immensely proud of her performance, and later wrote the spoken part of *Kaddish* for her. In addition, Felicia had trained as an actress and while she may not have been through the harshest of apprenticeships, her theatrical sensitivities were not eggshell delicate. Perhaps the unkindest display of Bernstein's temperament came when, anguished with the dreadful reception given to *1600 Pennsylvania Avenue*, he attacked Felicia for encouraging him to work with Alan Jay Lerner and reduced her to tears.

For the most part, Bernstein's liaisons with other (usually much younger) men had been discreet and short-lived, but the arrival of Thomas Cothran, accepted as part of the Bernstein 'family' household, marked an unhealthy departure. Stories vary, some of them suggesting that Felicia gave her husband an ultimatum; others, that he decided, in a fit of mid-life crisis, finally to 'come out' as a full, 'card-carrying' homosexual. In May of 1976, at the start of a six-week New York Philharmonic tour of the United States and Europe, he took Thomas Cothran with him, leaving Felicia at home.

Another of the Bernstein bicentennial commissions, set aside for the ill-fated *1600 Pennsylvania Avenue*, was a song cycle entitled *Songfest*, originally commissioned by the Philadelphia Orchestra, but now destined for the National Symphony Orchestra in Washington. Perhaps nostalgically recalling his youth, Bernstein read through anthologies of American poetry, Cothran at his side, and talked of renting a summer cottage on Long Island where they would work together. Felicia had returned with the family to Martha's Vineyard, where Cothran was not welcome.

In July 1976, following his son Alexander's twenty-first birthday, Bernstein moved out of his home. To avoid gossip, Harry Kraut persuaded him not to rent a house in Long Island but to find somewhere on the West Coast. Following some conducting engagements, Bernstein and Cothran rented a house for six weeks in Carmel, a little south of San Francisco. It was an unhappy period for both of the Bernsteins. Felicia smoked incessantly, could not sleep and, unwilling to accept the situation, told her friends that Leonard was working on the West Coast with Arthur Laurents. Leonard, apparently recapturing his golden youth and, in his own words, 'free at last', was, according to close friends, filled with guilt and uncertain of his future personal life. Nevertheless, the solitude helped him to complete four of the songs for *Songfest*.

On their return to New York, Bernstein and Cothran rented a suite in the Novarro Hotel, a few blocks from his home. Felicia had returned to the theatre, appearing in *Poor Murderer* by Pavel Kohout, with Maria Schell. Her estrangement from Bernstein had not been made public. They were seen dining together in the city and the announcement of their trial separation was not made until Bernstein had departed for Europe. Although the perennial 'grapevine' had always been aware of Bernstein's homosexual activities, the news of the break-up of New York's most glamorous couple was still a shock.

Bernstein had grown a moustache and beard in California and, looking somewhat Mosaic, he directed concerts in Munich on behalf of Amnesty International, and in Vienna, where he concluded Unitel's Mahler cycle. From there, he moved to Paris for further concerts and television. Cothran accompanied him wherever he went. In December, clean-shaven again, when speaking about Shostakovich's Fourteenth Symphony in a pre-concert talk at the New York Philharmonic, he referred obliquely to his break with his wife. Bernstein likened himself anomalously to Shostakovich when the Russian had been near death and expressing defiance of Soviet 'rules'. Bernstein concluded that an artist must free himself of all rules and restraints and live his life as he wants. They were brave words, but it is doubtful whether they were spoken with any great certainty. At the Inaugural Concert for President Carter the following month, Bernstein gave a preview of *Songfest*, with his setting of 'To My Dear and Loving Husband' by the seventeenth-century American poet Anne Bradstreet. Considering the current state of the Bernstein household, it was an unexpected choice.

Bernstein and Cothran spent the winter in Palm Springs, where his plan was to complete *Songfest*, prepare a series on music for BBC Television and start to assemble an opera based on Nabokov's *Lolita*. By February, however, he was back in New York. Being with Tom

Cothran permanently had proved to be impossible. Their ways of life did not blend and he wanted to return to Felicia.

In truth, Bernstein was too old and too set in his habits to adapt to a new lifestyle. Despite occasional pangs of guilt, idyllic evenings of poetry reading by the shores of the Pacific with a man half his age had been fun, but a diversion only. Cothran was bright, witty, musical, well-read and highly intelligent, but Bernstein was accustomed to a life tailor-made to his personal requirements. He had been spoiled and pampered for years and was not ready to accommodate another person's full-time presence. Felicia, in addition to her support, her understanding and constant encouragement, had raised and tended their children with care and love, also freeing him to live his 'public' life. She had created comfortable, stylish homes in New York and Connecticut, with an efficient entourage dedicated to her husband, and with servants and secretaries to attend his every need. Despite his wilful behaviour, she was an integral part of his life.

Their reconciliation was a gradual process. In March, they appeared together at the new Alice Tully Hall in Lincoln Center for a benefit concert, during which Felicia and Michael Wager, an old family friend, narrated *Façade*, Edith Sitwell's witty and occasionally gibberish poems set to music by William Walton. The New York press noted the event.

Bernstein continued his travels, with the English Bach Festival in London, the Israel Philharmonic (where Michael Wager narrated a revised text in 'Kaddish'), and recording for DGG in Vienna. Tom Cothran joined him for a brief (and, apparently, unhappy) holiday in Morocco, after which Bernstein travelled on to give a concert in Paris. Felicia was passing through the city, on her way to a holiday in Greece. Over the next months, they met regularly and by June were planning a holiday together in Austria, where there was to be a Bernstein Festival. They moved *en famille* to Tanglewood in July.

The happiness of the reunited family was shortlived. Felicia had been suffering from back pains and had also been troubled by a persistent cough, which she dismissed as a mild attack of bronchitis. She did not tell her husband who, after fulfilling a few more American concert obligations, flew to Austria to make their holiday arrangements. She did not join him. A bronchoscopy revealed that she had lung cancer.

Bernstein with his elder
daughter Jamie

Bernstein flew back to New York, moving into the family
apartment, and made all the necessary arrangements for his wife's
medical care. She began daily radiation treatments in New York and,
to avoid drawing attention to the gravity of his wife's illness, Bernstein
agreed to attend the Austrian festival in his honour, together with
several other public appearances he was scheduled to make. His work
took him from Villach in Austria to Berlin and Mainz, all with the
Israel Philharmonic, thence to the Salzburg Festival with the Vienna
Philharmonic. He spoke daily to Felicia and managed to steal three
free days, between Salzburg and Vienna, to be with her.

Felicia wanted to leave their Connecticut home (perhaps because it
held too many bad memories) and, in the autumn of the year,
Bernstein purchased a new house in East Hampton, Long Island.
Felicia endured regular chemotherapy treatments that were painful
and taxing. In October of the year, she was still well enough to
accompany her husband to Washington where, in the presence of
President Carter and his family, there was an all-Bernstein concert to
inaugurate Rostropovich as musical director of the National

Symphony. Bernstein gave the premières of *Slava!*, reworked from *1600 Pennsylvania Avenue*, and *Three Meditations*, for cello and orchestra, adapted from *Mass*. Rostropovich conducted the *On the Waterfront* suite and, after the interval, Bernstein conducted his newly finished *Songfest: A Cycle of American Poems for Six Singers and Orchestra*.

Bernstein always had a special affinity for vocal music, whether writing for the theatre or the concert hall, and his symphonies *Jeremiah* and *Kaddish* are greatly enhanced by his use of the voice. Apart from his contributions to the theatre, *Chichester Psalms* may yet emerge as his most enduring work. *Songfest*, which features twelve songs created from some of America's finest poetry, opens with a sextet, after which solos and various combinations take over (including two poems cleverly strung together as a duet) until the final joyful sextet. Coloured by Bernstein's diverse yet distinctively personal styles, including jazz and more than a hint of Broadway, it is one of his most open, delightful, touching, good-humoured and witty works, a far cry from the angst of *Kaddish*, the mysticism of *Dybbuk*, or the 'trendy' allusions of *Mass*. It celebrates America and American music.

The poems (which Tom Cothran helped Bernstein to select) were originally assembled as part of the bicentennial celebrations, and are as varied as the musical styles, providing a survey of some of America's best writers over a period of three hundred years of the country's history: Frank O'Hara, Lawrence Ferlinghetti, Julia de Burgos (from Puerto Rico), Walt Whitman, Langston Hughes and June Jordan (brilliantly combined), Anne Bradstreet, Gertrude Stein, e. e. cummings, Conrad Aiken, Gregory Corso, Edna St Vincent Millay and Edgar Allan Poe. Bernstein's personal favourite was 'What lips my lips have kissed' by Edna St Vincent Millay, in which the poet is haunted by thoughts of forgotten lovers, and it is perhaps the most deeply moving setting of the cycle.

As the year progressed, Felicia's health continued to deteriorate. An operation in November led to further heart complications the following month, but she travelled to Vienna – a city she had never really liked – in January of 1978, to be with her husband for a revival of *Fidelio* at the State Opera. She accompanied him to Milan for further performances of the same production at La Scala, before returning to New York for more treatment. Bernstein remained in

Opposite, Bernstein
celebrates his sixtieth
birthday with his friend
'Slava' (the conductor-cellist
Mstislav Rostropovich) and
the National Symphony
Orchestra of Washington DC,
25 August 1978.

Europe, travelling with the Vienna Philharmonic to London and
Paris, followed by two weeks with the Concertgebouw Orchestra in
Amsterdam.

In New York, Felicia's lung cancer had reached the stage where
surgery was not possible, and chemotherapy was the only and remote
hope. She moved to the new house on Long Island, with a bedroom
overlooking the sea. She had returned to the Catholic faith of her
childhood and a Mass was held in the room for her. On his return
from Europe, Bernstein cancelled all further engagements to be at
her side.

In the final weeks, she was sustained by powerful drugs, used to
reduce the pain, but which caused her mind to wander. She clung to
life for some days longer than the doctors and nurses predicted. Hour
by hour, fighting against the inevitable, she finally succumbed on
16 June 1978.

Throughout her life, Felicia had been a very heavy smoker, almost
as addicted as her husband, and there is little doubt that this was the
cause of her final illness. Bernstein, however, blamed himself for
Felicia's death. People who constantly repress their emotions,
particularly anger, are believed in some medical quarters to be more
vulnerable to cancer. In nearly twenty-seven years of marriage, Felicia
had hidden her true feelings beneath an elegantly serene mask, either
pretending not to notice her husband's libidinous homosexual
behaviour, his egocentric excesses and his narcissistic self-indulgences,
or accepting them as the failings of a wayward but brilliantly talented
man. Her frustrations increased over the years, as he became less
discreet in his amatory exploits, and they reached breaking-point with
the public humiliation of their separation. Bernstein carried the
burden of guilt for the rest of his life. Joan Peyser, a less sympathetic
observer, albeit an admirer, noted that Bernstein could only deal with
the situation by making himself the central character of the drama. He
grieved, she points out, but spoke only about *his own* obsessive guilt.

Following a period of mourning, Bernstein did not appear in
public until his sixtieth birthday, on 25 August. He would have
avoided the celebration in his honour, but it was being staged at Wolf
Trap, Washington's open-air concert stadium, to raise money for the
National Symphony Orchestra, which was seriously in debt. In
September, he buried himself again in work, conducting five

Beethoven symphonies for the Unitel cameras in Vienna, and giving the European première of *Songfest* in Munich. He was joined by Tom Cothran for some of the time, and there were further talks about the opera based on *Lolita*, but the project was again shelved.

After a Christmas spent in Jamaica, Bernstein officially represented the United States on behalf of Jimmy Carter by conducting the Mexico City Philharmonic Orchestra. He spent some time on holiday in Mexico, meeting the recently remarried Richard Burton and his wife in Puerto Vallarta. On his return to New York, he was troubled by a persistent throat virus, probably a souvenir of Mexico, which troubled him into the summer months, when he again toured Japan with the New York Philharmonic.

While he was in Japan, his desire to compose returned and he announced that 1980 would be another 'sabbatical' year, indicating only that he would set aside his usual demanding series of concert

A nostalgic reunion backstage at a revival of *West Side Story* in 1980. On Bernstein's right is Debbie Allen, who plays the part of the fiery Anita. On his left is Chita Rivera, who created the role in the 1957 production.

guest engagements in favour of periods for composing. His calendar was, however, as full as ever: Tanglewood, Israel, Salzburg, Hamburg, Vienna and Paris, with additional side visits to Positano to discuss an opera project with Zeffirelli and, at last, a triumphant appearance with Herbert von Karajan's Berlin Philharmonic Orchestra, to conduct a benefit performance of Mahler's Ninth Symphony on behalf of Amnesty International. There was a three-week Washington season in October with the Vienna State Opera and Vienna Philharmonic (which included five performances of Beethoven's *Fidelio*), followed by a concert performance of the opera with the New York Philharmonic.

By December, he was ready to leave the podium and embarked on two separate undertakings. The first was a musical film, with his old friends Comden and Green, about Preston Tucker, the pioneering car designer whose work was stifled by the established automobile giants of Detroit. Despite Francis Ford Coppola's patronage, the project fizzled out. The second, with Arthur Laurents, was a musical set in the Middle Ages, tentatively entitled *Alarums and Flourishes*, but it, too, was stillborn.

Bernstein was approaching the middle of 1980, his sabbatical year, and still had nothing to show for it. But in April he accepted a commission from the Boston Symphony, which was celebrating its centenary. With extra time on his hands and nostalgic memories in his heart, the result was the fifteen-minute *Divertimento*, a loving tribute to the city of his youth in eight short movements, in which the melodic motif B–C, also standing for Boston Centennial, always features. The eight vignettes – *Sennets and Tuckets* (a sennet is a Shakespearean signal call on a trumpet, and a tucket is a trumpet flourish), *Waltz, Mazurka, Samba, Turkey Trot* (a dance craze of the 1920s), *Sphinxes, Blues* and, finally, *March: 'The BSO Forever'* – are an indication of the light-hearted wit, musical puns and allusions and, above all, joyful reminiscences of a musical childhood. It is vintage Bernstein, lovingly crafted, with a gentle humour that seems to sweep aside all the sadness, the suffering, the guilt and the self-hatred of the preceding year. Around the time of the première, in late September of 1980, Bernstein referred to a Stravinsky dedication (the latter's *Symphony of Psalms*) which was 'to the glory of God and the Boston Symphony Orchestra', adding that if he dared put his name in the same league, he would dedicate his *Divertimento* 'To the Boston

Symphony Orchestra and my Mother', but might even go one better with a *triple* dedication – 'To the Boston Symphony Orchestra, my Mother, and Boston, my old home town.'

Divertimento is one of Bernstein's sunniest entertainments and augured well for the future, but the years to come rarely found him in such a happy state.

5

It's the artists of the world, the feelers and thinkers, who will ultimately save us, who can articulate, educate, defy, insist, sing and shout the big dreams. Only the artists can turn the 'Not-Yet' into reality.

Leonard Bernstein,
addressing students at Tanglewood

Returning an earlier compliment, Bernstein rehearses at the Kennedy Center in Washington for a concert honouring Rostropovich's sixtieth birthday.

The Final Decade 1980–90

Bernstein spoke frequently about Felicia in the years following her
death, claiming that not a day would pass without thoughts of her. He
missed her constantly. Those surrounding Bernstein also missed the
gentle restraint she had wielded over her often unruly husband.
Following in the Schuyler Chapin tradition, Harry Kraut was usually
there to maintain proprieties or smooth ruffled feathers, but his
charge was becoming increasingly difficult to manage. A devil-may-
care exhibitionism, mostly fuelled by whisky, led to frequent displays
of poor taste. In November of 1980, following a warm spoken
introduction to his old friend and mentor, Aaron Copland, there was
some delay before the elderly composer, enjoying his eightieth-
birthday celebrations, came on to the platform. Bernstein explained to
the audience that he 'went to pee'. It was not such a shocking thing to
say, but it was inappropriate and undignified.

Earlier the same evening Bernstein had made a fool of himself at a
black-tie reception at The Waldorf Hotel. Macmillan Publishers, in
the presence of the former Prime Minister, Harold Macmillan, were
launching their new and long-awaited twenty-volume edition of
Grove's Dictionary of Music and Musicians. Appropriately, the date of
the launch was 22 November, St Cecilia's Day (Cecilia being the
patron saint of music). Bernstein, who was clearly drunk, his clothes
dishevelled and his words slurred, launched into a long, meandering
diatribe, noting that the day was the seventeenth anniversary of the
death of his friend John F. Kennedy, and this had been ignored by
everyone, including the *New York Times*. He also talked about the
Profumo scandal, involving the notorious Christine Keeler, which had
led to the downfall of Sir Harold Macmillan's government. In the end,
one of the journalists tried to silence him, telling him he was talking
rubbish, but Bernstein insisted that the gathering should stand for two
minutes' silence in tribute to JFK.

Bernstein's own version of events was that Macmillan had given
him permission to talk about President Kennedy, but that he had been

Bernstein with his old friend
Aaron Copland during a
rehearsal of 'A Copland
Celebration!', a television
tribute to Copland in
recognition of his
eightieth birthday

heckled. It could also have been that the Grove article on his career
was bland and somewhat patronizing; and, as was so often the case,
it had singled out *West Side Story* as his most important musical
contribution.

Bernstein composed two further works in 1980. In the summer, he
wrote *Touches* for solo piano, subtitled *Chorale, Eight Variations and
Coda*, for contestants in the Van Cliburn International Piano
Competition in 1981. Being a pianist, he could compose a work that
would test the virtuosity of any keyboard hopeful. Later in the year he
composed *A Musical Toast*, dedicated to the memory of André
Kostelanetz, who had died in January. It is a light-hearted tribute to a

favourite New York conductor, former leader of New York's
Promenade Concerts (similar to the Boston Pops under Arthur
Fiedler), who had also commissioned a number of important works by
Copland (such as *Lincoln Portrait*), William Schuman and Alan
Hovhaness among others.

Bernstein was anxious to return to composing. He had formulated
the idea of creating a sequel to his one-act *Trouble in Tahiti*, having
always wondered what had happened to his characters in later years.
When he first wrote the opera, he had planned it as part of a larger
work, possibly a trilogy. Tom Cothran, with whom Bernstein had
maintained a regular correspondence, and who had been so
constructive in the creation of *Songfest*, might have been an ideal
collaborator in the project. But Cothran was taken seriously ill in
Japan and flew home to his parents in Chicago. (His affliction proved
to be an early example of AIDS.)

In October Bernstein received a request for an interview for the
magazine *Saturday Review*. It came from Stephen Wadsworth, who
had been at Harvard with Bernstein's daughter Jamie. Wadsworth's
request included a calculated attempt to intrigue Bernstein, in the
form of a P.S., asking whether he was interested in librettos. It
worked. Bernstein offered to trade his interview for the outline of a
sequel to *Trouble in Tahiti* (which had been composed before
Wadsworth was born). They met, and Bernstein was so impressed
with the 27-year-old that he decided he had found the right
collaborator, his superstitious nature aware that here was yet another
Stephen to complement Sondheim and Schwartz. After some
preliminary discussions, they mapped out a family history
that would make the darkest Eugene O'Neill drama look positively
tame. Extended conducting duties at home and overseas, however,
occupied much of 1981. The interview for *Saturday Review* was
never written.

In New York, Bernstein gave the première of new works by Ned
Rorem and Lukas Foss, as well as directing a retrospective of Aaron
Copland's music. In Israel, with Jean-Pierre Rampal as soloist, he gave
the first performance of *Halil*, a nocturne for solo flute, string
orchestra and percussion. Composed during the winter of 1980–81,
Halil (the Hebrew word for 'flute') is dedicated 'to the spirit of Yadin
and his fallen brothers'. Yadin Tenenbaum was an Israeli flautist killed

in the 1973 war, and although Bernstein never met him, he said, 'I know his spirit.' Once again, Bernstein uses the conflict between tonal and non-tonal music to express the struggle between the anguish of war and the desire to live in peace, and the work alternately moves between an angular twelve-tone row and moments of great lyricism. Borrowing the language of the Hungarian composer Béla Bartók, the 'Nocturne' of his title is Bartókian 'night-music', in which, according to the composer, there is 'an on-going conflict of nocturnal images: wish-dreams, nightmares, repose, sleeplessness, night terrors – and sleep itself, *Death's twin brother* ...' In this last description, Bernstein might have been describing his own troubled feelings. A lifelong insomniac, he suffered constantly from sleepless nights, rarely achieving respite before the dawn hours.

As with so many of Bernstein's works, there is a definite programme. After episodes in the finale that are described as 'shrieking' and 'crude' (the horrors of war), the solo flute is silent, suggesting the death of the protagonist. But it is also, as ever, a work that can be fully appreciated without reference to programme notes. *Halil* – only sixteen minutes long and played without pause – is an immediately accessible and appealing flute concerto, frequently programmed by orchestras around the world.

At the Vatican, Bernstein gave a performance of *Kaddish* for the Pope, and it would be fascinating to know how the pontiff reacted to a work that had been damned as 'sacrilegious' less than twenty years earlier. Throughout the year, Bernstein also gave recorded concert performances of Wagner's *Tristan und Isolde*, an opera that had fascinated him for most of his life. The original plan, to record each of its three acts on separate occasions during different periods of the year, giving the singers time to regain their strength, was ideal. Unfortunately, Bernstein and the cast, headed by Peter Hofmann and Hildegard Behrens, were dogged by ill health on each occasion, but the final recording – pieced together from rehearsals as well as the concerts – reveals an outstanding and spacious performance.

During the summer months, Bernstein and Wadsworth settled to the task of creating the continuation of *Trouble in Tahiti*, familiarly known as *TinT II*, and were confident that they were making enough satisfactory progress for Harry Kraut to begin negotiations with three opera houses – the Houston Grand Opera, the Kennedy Center and

The unmistakeable profile, caricatured by John Minnion

La Scala, Milan – to share the costs of commissioning the music and setting up the production.

The original story had ended with Dinah and Sam (to avoid talking to one another) on their way to see *Trouble in Tahiti*, a dreadful South Sea Island epic, at their local cinema. The sequel, which carries a number of uneasy references to the lives of Bernstein and even Wadsworth, is a dark echo of the brittle, bitter-sweet portrait of American suburbia in 1952. When the story resumes, thirty years have passed. Dinah has recently died in a drunken car crash. (In the previous year, Wadsworth's much loved sister had been killed in an automobile accident.) At Bernstein's suggestion, Sam and Dinah's son, Junior, who did not appear in the first opera, has grown up to be a psychotic homosexual, unable to communicate with his father. In addition, there is now a younger sister, Dede, about whom Junior has incestuous fantasies. (Bernstein's enemies hinted, over the years, that he had an unhealthy relationship with his sister Shirley, although such assertions never went beyond ugly gossip.) The play's Dede is married to François, a French-Canadian, who has been – and maybe still is – Junior's lover.

Bernstein and Wadsworth added other characters who, for those playing biographical detective games, could be linked to real life. One of Dinah's mourners, Mrs Doc, claims to have been in love with her. She might well be a recreation of Lillian Hellman, a close friend of the Bernsteins for many years. Hellman fell out bitterly with Leonard over her ill-fated *Candide* book, but remained forever loyal to Felicia, even casting a shadow over Bernstein's televised sixtieth-birthday celebrations by talking about his late wife's final suffering. But whether or not these allusions were real or imagined, *TinT II* presented a murky, unpromising portrait of a dysfunctional family.

When the summer ended, Bernstein returned to the podium for three months, mainly to conduct Brahms in Vienna and Wagner in Munich. By January of 1982, he was able to return to composing while in residence at a new Institute for Advance Study in Bloomington, Indiana. In addition to social duties, he gave conducting classes and even tried out some of his new operatic material during student workshop sessions.

Composing was further interrupted in the spring, with the successful American première of *Halil*, performed by the National

Bernstein celebrates at the Salzburg Summer Festival with Claudio Abbado (left) and James Levine.

Symphony in Washington. A little later, Bernstein travelled to England, where further displays of self-indulgence and a wilfully slow performance of Elgar's *Enigma Variations* failed to win over members of the BBC Symphony Orchestra, the press or the audience. Backstage, Bernstein was heard boastfully dismissing the conducting of Sir Adrian Boult and 'Eddie' Elgar (a quaint diminutive nobody had used before), claiming that he alone understood what the music was about. In Israel, he conducted Stravinsky for the composer's centennial year, recorded his own works for DGG, then led the orchestra on a tour that included West Germany, Mexico and Texas. Further travels occupied his time until the end of June.

In July, his love affair with the Boston Symphony and Tanglewood officially ended, and he travelled to Los Angeles to create a West Coast version of the school that he had once helped Koussevitzky establish in the Berkshire hills. The trouble dated back a year, to 1981, when the orchestra's players had complained about an all-Bernstein Independence Day concert. They disliked his new music, were scornful of playing 'show tunes' and were impatient with his long-winded rehearsals. Bernstein, prevented from making a new recording of Gershwin's *Rhapsody in Blue*, castigated both orchestra and management in a local New York paper and cancelled his winter appearances during the Boston Symphony's centennial season. Los Angeles, however, could not match the atmosphere offered by the sylvan settings of Tanglewood (and, almost certainly, the nostalgic memories it evoked). Bernstein supervised conducting studies, and recorded *Rhapsody in Blue*. The West Coast première of *Songfest*, given in an open-air concert where the words were often inaudible, was a failure. Feeling somewhat depressed, Bernstein had set aside more time to work with Stephen Wadsworth, but bronchial flu sent him home instead, and he was needed in Vienna by early September for more filming.

When he returned, another metamorphosis of *Candide* was presented at the State Theater in Lincoln Center. Again with a book (further expanded) by Hugh Wheeler, directed by Harold Prince and conducted by John Mauceri, it was slowly moving towards the final version that Bernstein sought, but even though it was enormously successful, it had not yet reached its destination.

Late in 1982, Bernstein was able to go back to work on the opera, now called *A Quiet Place*, a poignant phrase that had appeared in *Trouble in Tahiti* (and had also been used, with Bernstein's permission, as the title of a short-lived stage play by Julian Claman, starring Tyrone Power). After Bernstein's usual delays and diversions, he and Wadsworth were facing a deadline, set for June of 1983, in Houston, Texas. Bernstein worked through the winter months, eschewing his usual holidays in the sun, and had enough material by the spring of 1983 for student workshop try-outs at Juilliard. Gordon Davidson, who had become Bernstein's most regular stage director, turned down the assignment, which finally went to Peter Mark Schifter, and a Bernstein Tanglewood student, John De Main, was chosen to conduct the new production.

Bernstein, who had been both generous and supportive of his young collaborator (although he accepted that Wadsworth was not experienced enough to direct the first production), kept up his spirits during the trials of the final rehearsals with charming notes and poems slipped under the door of the younger man's hotel room at various hours of the night. One of them stated (of the opera), 'It's also a thing of despair and of fright, which *no one* will love on opening night!' His dark prophesy was venomously fulfilled after the production opened to much fanfare on 17 June 1983. There were a number of cruel reviews from important critics, one of whom wrote that it rang false, comparing it with a soap opera. 'Pretentious failure' were key words. Another launched a personal attack on Bernstein, speaking of 'a prodigious talent in decline'. Andrew Porter in *The New Yorker* was reassuringly favourable, likening the double-bill (the original production featured *Trouble in Tahiti* as the first half, with the new material as the second) to an American *Ring*, 'played out … in a Great Neck [a New York suburb] home'.

Whether or not they had anticipated a majority 'thumbs-down', Bernstein and Wadsworth agreed that more work was needed on the opera, and postponed the October performances at the Kennedy Center until the following year, after the Milan production. One of the major problems to be solved was that the acerbic caricature of American suburbia in *Trouble in Tahiti* – complete with an Andrews-Sisters-style close harmony group extolling the virtues of the 'little white house' – established the wrong mood for the gothic melodrama of the second part. Furthermore, in an over-long evening, the interval between the two operas came too soon.

John Mauceri, who was to conduct both the Scala and Washington performances, came up with solutions to some of the problems. *Trouble in Tahiti*, divided into two parts, was used in flashback sequences during Act II, and some of the material was cut, to make the evening shorter overall. The new version, directed by Stephen Wadsworth, was well received by the Italian press in June of 1984. It was followed a month later by the Kennedy Center production, which still failed to please the majority of reviewers. In 1986, Bernstein conducted a production at the Vienna State Opera, which was both recorded and televised.

Bernstein's music from two composing eras, separated by thirty years, never really blends satisfactorily and the plot seems to resolve itself more by accident than design. In its final version, it opens with the funeral of Dinah, during which one is made aware of the tragic underlying tensions between the family members. Later the same evening, Sam (the father) reads his late wife's diaries, which trigger memories and a flashback to *Trouble in Tahiti*. Back in the present, the daughter Dede seeks closeness to her father, while Junior and François fight, and Junior fantasizes about his incestuous relationship with Dede. Dede and François (her husband) are reconciled with one another, and Sam goes into the bedroom, where his son is sleeping, hoping to achieve some sort of reconciliation of his own. A trophy on a shelf – a somewhat clumsy ploy – reawakens further memories, and the scene shifts back to a sequence in *Trouble in Tahiti*, when Sam had missed going to Junior's school play because he was preoccupied with competing in a handball tournament.

In the final act, Dede is working in the garden her late mother loved to tend. She is joined by Junior, and they indulge in remembered children's games, also recalling their parents' breakfast-time quarrels. François and, later, Sam join them in games of 'tag', during which Sam is seen to welcome François to the family. He reads from Dinah's diary and a small disagreement leads to a vicious argument, ending when Junior hurls the diary into the air, making the pages scatter and fall. Remembering Dinah's words, they realize that they must communicate with one another and, in a mood similar to the finale of *Mass*, they reach out to each other.

Perhaps the plot fails to convince or move many audiences because there is nothing heroic or even particularly endearing about any of the characters involved. Bernard Holland, in the *New York Times*, felt that Bernstein had squandered his prodigious talents on the characters, whose 'sufferings repel rather than move.' Some of the music, particularly the orchestral sequences, echoes Bernstein's deeply emotional involvement. It is intense and often moving, but there are long portions where one is left with the feeling that he is simply accommodating a self-conscious libretto.

Bernstein must have been disappointed that he had failed to create 'The Great American Opera', but he was accustomed to being attacked by the press, fairly or unfairly, and was surrounded by a close coterie of admirers who could reassure him. After the death of Felicia, his personal attachments were homosexual, but he did not live in a self-consciously gay community, even though it was a fashionable time to 'come out'. His personal popularity with the public was never higher, and continuing reports of his misbehaviour, drunken displays and lack of self-discipline were mostly restricted to the gossipy confines of the music world.

The public, however, saw some of the maestro's less appealing characteristics in the television broadcast of a documentary film about the DGG recording of a new version of *West Side Story*, with an inappropriate 'all-star' operatic cast. While Bernstein understandably wanted to hear his music sung by some of the finest voices of the time, the casting of the New Zealander Kiri Te Kanawa as the Puerto Rican Maria and the markedly accented Spaniard José Carreras as the all-American Tony was faintly ridiculous. But the supporting roles, played by Kurt Ollmann and Tatiana Troyanos (a New Yorker who could perfectly mimic the Puerto Rican accent almost to a degree of caricature), were excellently played, and the New York pick-up studio musicians, a legendary breed, provided a musical backing that no pit orchestra in the world could match.

The interviews with the performers were entertaining if a little fulsome. Working with Bernstein was, according to Carreras, 'a dream'. (At the sessions, it turned out to be a nightmare.) Kiri Te Kanawa likened it to having Mozart there, although it might have been more appropriate if her comparison had been with singing *Porgy and Bess* for the Gershwin brothers.

A fly-on-the-wall technique was used to sit in on the recording sessions, at which Bernstein displayed some of his worst 'playing to the gallery' antics. Those who had witnessed Bernstein in the recording studio before knew a little of what to expect, with the maestro generally complaining about everything (but never admitting that he was ill-prepared), 'emoting', talking instead of conducting, causing hold-ups, disagreements and general chaos; then, when all seemed lost, riding in like the cavalry to save the day, and carrying the recording to a successful conclusion.

As usual, he battered his long-suffering and ever-faithful record producer, John McClure (who had worked with him since the early 1960s), with petty complaints and offensive criticisms. He needled Carreras over his musical as well as his linguistic abilities, to the point that the tenor could ill conceal his rage and frustration, and generally played the role of wounded Jewish mother, driven to an early grave by churlish, ungrateful children. Needless to say, it made wonderfully entertaining television, which, to the uninitiated viewer, showed the 'genius' Leonard Bernstein winning through against seemingly impossible odds.

The showing of the film had an enormously beneficial influence on the marketing of the recording. The casting of both Te Kanawa and Carreras was questioned by more than a few critics, but it was nevertheless an excellent recording, with wonderful instrumental playing, first-class chorus work and, leaving aside an odd assortment of accents (often acceptable in an opera house), some fine singing. One Bernstein biographer noted that commercial considerations had outweighed artistic ones, and believed that such a decision was 'a bad one'. It is unlikely that DGG's executives agreed, as the album became one of the company's all-time bestsellers.

Two other BBC television programmes showed Bernstein in a better light, and again revealed his skills as teacher and communicator. *The Little Drummer Boy*, a documentary about the life and music of Gustav Mahler, and *The Love of Three Orchestras*, a tribute to the New York, Israel and Vienna Philharmonic orchestras, made excellent viewing.

During the final decade of his life, Bernstein was constantly torn between the public demand for his appearances as a conductor and his own desire to compose. At a fifty-fifth birthday party in his honour during the Edinburgh Festival, as far back as 1973, he had wept genuine tears, induced perhaps by a generous intake of whisky, noting that he *still* had no masterpiece by which to be remembered. In 1985 the anguish remained, and there is little doubt that he realized that *A Quiet Place* would never be a suitable memorial. A year earlier, in the summer following the Washington performances, he had discussed a new project with Stephen Wadsworth, suggesting a multilingual opera that would outline the decline of western society. He was looking for a *magnum opus* with which to make a major statement about the future of the world, and one in which, like so many of his works, faith would eventually triumph. By May 1985, Wadsworth had developed a scenario for a three-act opera, tracing the history of the world since the Holocaust, but it failed to spark Bernstein's imagination, leaving him deeply depressed.

In the summer of 1985, Bernstein did begin to compose one new work. *Jubilee Games*, in two movements, was written for the Israel Philharmonic, which was to celebrate its fiftieth anniversary in 1986. It was a work in progress. Written in a hurry and, because of the usual time pressures, with help in the orchestration from Jack Gottlieb and Sid Ramin, he planned additional movements at a later date.

Opposite, a portrait by Don Hunstein, who photographed Bernstein for nearly forty years

Peace and an end to world tensions, however, remained the prevailing thought in Bernstein's mind, motivating many of his activities. In 1985, his contribution took the form of a Journey for Peace with the European Community Youth Orchestra, beginning in Athens, and continuing to Hiroshima in August to mark the fortieth anniversary of the dropping of the first atomic bomb. His programme, which was conducted by a protégé, Eiji Oue, included a new *Hiroshima Requiem* by the Japanese woman composer Tomiko Köjiba, as well as a Mozart violin concerto played by the child prodigy Midori and Bernstein's own *Kaddish* Symphony. After Hiroshima, the orchestra repeated the programme in Budapest and Vienna on their way home.

Within days, Bernstein was in Schleswig-Holstein, to help Justus Frantz set up a new festival, then on to Tel Aviv and the Israel Philharmonic, with whom he embarked on a second Japanese tour within a month. It was a typical Bernstein undertaking, requiring vast resources of energy that would tax a much younger – and fitter – man. By the autumn, he was back in Vienna, filming Schumann and embarking upon a new Shostakovich cycle. He returned to Vienna in the spring of 1986 to conduct *A Quiet Place* at the State Opera, then took part in a Bernstein Festival in London directed by John Mauceri. After that came honours in Paris (the Légion d'Honneur) and

A scene from the Vienna State Opera's production of *A Quiet Place*; the opera went through numerous revisions before the final version was presented in Vienna.

Munich (the Hartmann medal), conducting Haydn's *The Creation* at the first Schleswig-Holstein festival (as well as conducting classes), and a return to New York for appearances with the Philharmonic.

The two-movement *Jubilee Games* received its première in the autumn of 1986, a time which also marked the start of another conducting marathon. He began a Sibelius cycle in Vienna, recorded Puccini's *La bohème* in Rome and, working through to 1987, recorded five Mahler symphonies, sharing them between the Concertgebouw in Amsterdam, the New York Philharmonic and Vienna.

The departure of Stephen Wadsworth as a collaborator left Bernstein again without a composing project to spur his imagination. Jerome Robbins persuaded him to reconsider Brecht's *The Exception and the Rule*, renamed *The Race to Urga*, working with John Guare but, after a flurry of activity in early 1987, the project was dropped.

In early spring, Thomas Cothran, who had been critically ill for many months, died of AIDS. Some months before, Bernstein and Harry Kraut had organized a benefit concert for medical research, which raised $300,000. Later in 1987, they organized the first 'Music for Life' AIDS benefit at Carnegie Hall, which raised $1,700,000.

The AIDS virus, which so cruelly diminished America's homosexual population during the 1980s, took the life of another close friend, Jack Romann of the Baldwin Piano Company. In April 1988, Bernstein composed the song suite *Arias and Barcarolles* for a fund-raising concert dedicated to him. Its title was, ironically, taken from an ill-informed comment made by President Eisenhower many years earlier. Having heard Bernstein perform *Rhapsody in Blue* at a White House concert, the ex-general had voiced a preference for music with a good tune, without all those 'arias and barcarolles'! The work, originally for vocal quartet and two pianos, contains seven songs and an epilogue (dedicated to his mother), and is a lighthearted and partly autobiographical 'seven ages of man'.

The first song is borrowed from material he wrote to celebrate his daughter Jamie's wedding, the second presents some familiar comments from his life: 'What shall we call the baby?' and, even more appropriately, 'Why can't I give up smoking?'. 'Little Smary' remembers a bedtime story (Bernstein credits his mother for the text), and 'The Love of My Life' is dedicated to Stephen Wadsworth and Kurt Ollmann. 'Greeting' was originally written following the birth of

During the Deutsche
Grammophon recording of
Puccini's *La bohème* in Rome,
Bernstein is pictured with
(left to right) James Busterud,
Paul Plishka, Gimi Beni, Barbara
Daniels and Paul Kreider.

his son Alexander, and the sixth song is a setting by a contemporary Yiddish poet, about a *klezmer* who plays at a wedding. The final song, 'Mr and Mrs Webb Say Goodnight', is named after the Dean of Indiana University, and makes use of a lyric that Betty Comden had drafted for the stillborn *Tucker* musical. At the first performance, Bernstein and Michael Tilson Thomas played the two pianos, for what Bernstein described as 'a work in progress'. It was later revised for two singers for an official première in Israel the following year and, later still, orchestrated by the Chinese composer Bright Sheng, with a little help from Bernstein, for his final Tanglewood concert in 1990. (Sadly, Bernstein was not well enough to conduct it himself, and the orchestral première was given in his presence by Carl St Clair, the Boston Symphony's resident Assistant Conductor.)

While Bernstein's future composing plans remained unresolved in May of 1988, he at least had the satisfaction of seeing his wayward brain-child *Candide* restored to the form he had always hoped for. Once again, it was thanks to John Mauceri, whose contributions to Bernstein's later works are immeasurable. Now music director of Scottish Opera in Glasgow, Mauceri invited the multi-talented Jonathan Miller (whose own professional career had begun as a satirist in the pioneering *Beyond the Fringe*) to direct, together with the English writer John Wells who, with Miller, would revise dialogue and add some new scenes based on the original novella. The broad farce of the Hugh Wheeler–Harold Prince productions would be replaced with something closer to Voltaire's mercurial wit. The result was enormously successful, and the production was later staged at London's Old Vic.

Some recent wounds were healed in the summer of 1988, when the Boston Symphony Orchestra held a four-day celebration at Tanglewood in honour of Bernstein's seventieth birthday. Musicians from around the world composed and performed works in his honour, and students played his *Jeremiah* Symphony and *Mass*. Seiji Ozawa, Michael Tilson Thomas and Leon Fleisher conducted some of his favourite music. There was a gala concert on 25 August, and Bernstein's ninety-year-old mother, still going strong, was guest of honour at a pre-concert cocktail party. There were videotaped messages from around the world, and the special programme was filled with tributes from close friends and family.

A meeting of two veteran 'songsmiths': Jule Styne, aged eighty-two, hugs Bernstein on his seventieth birthday.

Further celebrations were held in Vienna a month later, and he was made an honorary citizen of the State of Austria. A poem that he wrote at the time reveals darker feelings: unhappiness with the passage of time and its accompanying physical discomforts (he was being treated for a prostate condition). When he had deserted Felicia for Tom Cothran twelve years earlier, she had angrily predicted that he would die a bitter and lonely old man. This was not to happen, but, surfeited with adulation and left alone in his hotel to suffer 'all the spooks of swift-advancing age', Bernstein likened himself to the Marschallin in *Der Rosenkavalier* who, after permanently dismissing her young lover Octavian, goes alone for a ride in Vienna's Prater.

In the autumn, Bernstein returned to conduct the New York Philharmonic in a series of concerts that promoted the work of fellow American composers David del Tredici, Charles Ives and Ned Rorem, as well as a three-movement version of *Jubilee Games*, to which he had added an *Opening Prayer*, for baritone solo and orchestra, originally composed in 1986 for the reopening of Carnegie Hall, as a second movement (the work was still not complete).

Before retiring to Florida for the winter months, he travelled to Cambridge University for a performance of the first British production (under difficult conditions) of *A Quiet Place*, staying in the country long enough to see and celebrate the brilliant Scottish production of *Candide* in its London début. February of 1989 brought the sad news of the death of the ever-faithful Helen Coates, aged eighty-nine. For more than half a century, she had created and maintained a Bernstein archive, and had watched her enthusiastic teenage piano student emerge as the most important classical music personality in the world.

In April that year, Bernstein travelled to Israel to conduct the première of his finished, four-movement *Jubilee Games*, now retitled Concerto for Orchestra. Throughout his career, he had been criticized for being a 'reactionary' composer, but the accusations were misinformed. Bernstein wrote from the heart in the eclectic American style that he developed over many years and, although he did not choose to become part of the latest musical fashion, he still experimented. Aleatory music (taken from the Latin *aleator*: a dice thrower) had been around for centuries. It is 'music of chance' and has

A late portrait by Christina Burton – the wrinkles grow deeper but the smile remains.

taken many forms. Mozart wrote a musical game in which twelve interchangeable musical phrases could be chosen at random from a throw of dice. Early in the twentieth century, Charles Ives experimented with chance and improvisation and, in the 1960s, a number of leading composers, notably Pierre Boulez, composed aleatory works. (The pages of one of his piano sonatas, for example, are held by a ring-binder, and the performer may start from any place, continuing until returning to the 'start' position. In his *Pli Selon Pli*, some pages of the score are divided into four separate sections, and the conductor may choose the sequence in which the orchestra performs them.) It was only natural that Bernstein, a man who loved crosswords, anagrams, word games and puzzles, would try his hand at such musical mental gymnastics. In *Dybbuk*, he had already experimented with eight-tone (octatonic) scales, instead of the traditional scale of seven or twelve notes, and had used mysterious anagrams and numerology as a musical extension of the metaphysical powers of the *Kabbalah*.

Bernstein introduced both aleatory and numerological techniques into Concerto for Orchestra, the origin of which was the celebration of the fiftieth anniversary of the Israel Philharmonic. According to Biblical injunction, every fiftieth year is celebrated with the sounding of the ram's horn (*shofar*) and the work opens with horn calls while players in the orchestra shout *sheva* (number 'seven' in Hebrew) seven times, followed by *hamishim* ('fifty') to acknowledge the fiftieth birthday. In addition, the players improvise their parts, sometimes playing to the accompaniment of pre-recorded tapes. This first movement is called *Free-Style Events*, suggesting the *Jubilee Games* of the original title. The second movement, entitled *Mixed Doubles*, presents a theme and variations of much greater simplicity; there are some unusual couplings of instruments, such as flute with horn, trumpet with double bass, clarinet and trombone, timpani and percussion instruments, and alto flute and bass clarinet. The theme on which the variations are based is built upon an octatonic scale that Bernstein used in his *Dybbuk* ballet. Since Bernstein had changed the title of the work to Concerto for Orchestra, also the name of a work by Bartók that Bernstein greatly admired and frequently conducted, it has been suggested that he might have been inspired by the Hungarian composer's second movement *Giuoco delle coppie* ('Play of

Couples'). The third movement, *Diaspora Dances*, involves some complicated mathematics combined with *gematria* (assigning numerical values to each letter of the Hebrew alphabet.) The first dance tune is in 18/8 time, and the orchestra whispers the words *hai* and *hayyim* (meaning 'alive' and 'life'). This unusual metre was chosen because the Hebrew letters of the words *hai*, 'alive', also form the numerical equivalent of eighteen (and *Le'hayim,* 'to life!', is the traditional drinking toast). Further complications include mathematical allusions to the founding of the orchestra in 1936, the number of 'just men' that God requires in each generation, groups of beats and metrical blocks. What emerges, however, are delightful, rhythmic dances that recall Bernstein's own Hasidic origins and, in his words, 'a New Yorkish kind of jazz'.

The final movement, originally used for Carnegie Hall, is entitled *Benediction*, and is very typical of Bernstein's 'thoughtful' style; in it the singer intones (in Hebrew) words from the Book of Numbers that are equally familiar to the Christian world: 'May the Lord bless you and keep you. May the Lord make His face to shine upon you and be gracious unto you. May the Lord lift up His countenance upon you and give you peace.' As ever, Bernstein's final message called for peace.

In June of 1989, Bernstein returned to his Holocaust project, now working with John Wells, who had done so much to restore *Candide* with Jonathan Miller. The new working title of the project was *Babel*. Sadly, nothing concrete ever developed. He approached other writers – Peter Shaffer and John Guare – who offered little encouragement, and the Holocaust project remained locked inside Bernstein's head.

After a quiet Tanglewood, Bernstein travelled to Poland, to share in concerts marking the fiftieth anniversary of World War II. From there, he returned to Vienna where, in addition to recordings, he conducted a memorial concert for Herbert von Karajan. In New York, all-Copland followed by all-Tchaikovsky concerts with the Philharmonic drew plaudits from the press, which had at last come to recognize him as a master conductor.

In December 1989 – a month that saw unimagined political upheavals across Europe – Bernstein was in London to conduct and record his 'final' version of *Candide*, with the London Symphony Orchestra. An all-star cast was headed by Jerry Hadley (Candide) and

June Anderson (Cunegonde) and with Adolph Green as the philosopher Dr Pangloss. It was to be a similar exercise to the *West Side Story* recording, but with more appropriate casting. A flu epidemic mercilessly attacked the cast, including Bernstein, but the performances and the recording survived.

The final version takes Candide, the illegitimate nephew of Baron Thunder-Ten-Tronck, tutored by Dr Pangloss, loved by Cunegonde, through wonderfully complicated adventures that start in Westphalia, then to Lisbon (where they are arrested as heretics and brought to the auto-da-fé to face the Grand Inquisitor), to Paris, by sea to Buenos Aires, into the South American jungle, to the legendary Eldorado, to Surinam, then the Casino in Venice and, finally, a small farm outside the floating city. Having survived, Candide and Cunegonde, 'neither

Leonard Bernstein first met Adolph Green at a summer camp in 1937, where they staged a production of *The Pirates of Penzance*. Their last collaboration was in 1989, when Green took part in the recording of the final version of *Candide*.

Bernstein recording *Candide* at the EMI Studios in Abbey Road, London

pure, nor wise nor good', will do their best, build their house and 'make our garden grow'.

Throughout the final version of this magnificent play-with-music/musical/operetta/light opera, the lyrics dazzle and delight and Bernstein's score is witty, amusing, satirical, sentimental, touching and even deeply moving. *Candide* survived all its adaptations, alterations and metamorphoses to emerge as a triumphant creation. Like any work of art, its message is universal, with continuing verities that are applicable to all times. It is a unique contribution to the musical theatre of this century.

A few days after the London recording, Bernstein flew to Berlin to help celebrate its restoration as an undivided city. Still suffering from his London flu bout, he conducted Beethoven's Ninth Symphony at West Berlin's Philharmonie Hall on 23 December, and at East Berlin's Schauspielhaus on Christmas Day. To suit the occasion, and to underline the euphoria of the moment, he changed the words of Schiller's 'Ode to Joy' in the fourth movement from *Freude* ('Joy') to *Freiheit* ('Freedom'), making Beethoven's masterpiece an 'Ode to Freedom'. It was an unforgettable musical contribution to a turning-point in modern history.

Exhausted and still suffering the after-effects of flu, Bernstein beat a retreat to Key West in Florida, for rest and, possibly, work with John Wells on *Babel*. He was in no shape to work, however, and his home was constantly filled with visitors: friends and family, or associates with new plans and projects. He also enjoyed the closeness and friendship of his latest male 'constant companion', of whom there had been a number over the preceding years. Rest and sunshine helped enormously, but he did not recuperate as quickly as usual. In mid January, he cancelled a brief visit to New York to hear the Empire Brass Quintet perform his Dance Suite at the fiftieth anniversary celebrations of the American Ballet Theatre (the suite was reworkings of some sketches written in the past and put away in a drawer for some future occasion – Bernstein never threw any of his music away). He finally returned to the city in February, but did not feel well enough to undertake a conducting engagement at the Curtis Institute. He left for Vienna, for two weeks of conducting and recording, then returned with the Vienna Philharmonic to give three concerts at Carnegie Hall.

The punishing schedule continued, with a further European trip to conduct Mozart's C minor Mass with the Bavarian Radio Symphony Orchestra and Chorus in an eighteenth-century church in a small town north of Munich. During the filming, he used the opportunity of an introductory talk to discuss the pointlessness of war and, in a changing Europe, a more optimistic hope for peace. On his return to Munich, he made an additional journey, at the invitation of Wagner's granddaughter, to visit the opera house at Bayreuth and the villa 'Wahnfried' where Wagner had lived.

Bernstein gave two more performances of the Mozart Mass in Munich, then flew to Paris for an evening of his concert films at the Louvre, continuing on to Boston the next day in time to celebrate Passover with his mother. Once he was back in New York, however, there was new concern over his health. During the trip, he had been experiencing back pains that seemed to be similar to those suffered by Felicia at an early stage of her illness. Fearing the worst, tests were made, and a malignant but curable tumour was found on the membrane surrounding his lung. Treatment would take the form of radiation therapy.

The news of his treatment never reached the press and, a few weeks later, Bernstein was considered well enough to travel to Prague, where he appeared during the famous 'Prague Spring' festival, met with President Havel, and conducted Beethoven's Ninth Symphony to conclude the festivities, once again substituting the word *Freiheit* for *Freude*. It was a different conductor, however, from the hedonistic Bernstein of old, ready to party all night. After the concert, the door to his dressing-room was firmly closed to all visitors. Radiation treatment had left scars on his chest. His Viennese lawyer, Fritz Willheim, had brought oxygen supplies, in case of a recurrence of emphysema, and a New York acupuncturist was part of the travelling party.

Bernstein's return to New York revealed new physical problems. While the radiation treatment had been effective, it had caused an accumulation of fluid in the area of his lungs, requiring further hospital treatment. Other drugs were administered, against which Bernstein's system reacted badly, causing painful skin rashes. His sister Shirley took him home to Fairfield, Connecticut to recuperate, but he was less than two weeks away from his next – and important – undertaking. The first Pacific Music Festival (originally planned for

Beijing, but transferred to Sapporo in Japan after the brutal events of Tiananmen Square) was set to begin. He had arranged to conduct two concerts with the London Symphony Orchestra, and a further one with the festival's student orchestra, whose players were from twenty-three countries. There were conducting classes and, following the inaugural concerts in the Art Park outside Sapporo, additional performances in Tokyo (in the presence of the Emperor and Empress of Japan) and Osaka.

Against his doctors' advice, Bernstein travelled to Sapporo. Harry Kraut ensured that he was given every possible care, but the journey to Japan was a nightmare for the conductor, who was in constant pain and unable to sleep. Somehow, after three short days of recuperation, Bernstein took part in the opening ceremonies. He was still weak and his speech faltered, but he managed.

Having difficulty with his breathing, and taking pain-killing drugs, Bernstein rehearsed the two orchestras, seeming to draw new strength from working with the students. As if defying the powers of nature, he joined his friends for evening meals and receptions, celebrating with all his old verve, and playing host at an Independence Day party. His health had deteriorated by the time they reached Tokyo, but he conducted the London Symphony before the Emperor and Empress in the famous Suntory Hall. Now surviving on pain-killers and, in the words of his assistant, Craig Urquhart, 'doing his *danse macabre*', Bernstein gave a second concert with the London orchestra. He was still faced with an open-air arena concert, conducting the combined orchestras of the London Symphony and the Pacific Music Festival. Two days later, Bernstein collapsed. Further appearances were cancelled, and Michael Tilson Thomas and Eiji Oue took over the remaining concerts. The press announcement stated that Bernstein was suffering from exhaustion, not having fully recovered from ailments suffered in the spring.

With the wisdom of hindsight, one could say that Bernstein should never have undertaken the Japanese tour. On the other hand, his health had deteriorated to such a degree that the strain probably did little additional serious damage. The trip gave him a final opportunity to see old friends and colleagues in the Far East. It also gave one more generation of young musicians the experience and the personal contact with a musical 'citizen of the world' whose example would be an inspiration for the rest of their lives.

Bernstein retired again to his home in Fairfield. It was mid July and, within a month, he was expected in Tanglewood for a week with the student orchestra. After that, the annual Koussevitzky Memorial concert with the Boston Symphony would be followed by a week-long European tour with the student orchestra, to celebrate the fiftieth anniversary of the Berkshire Music Center. His doctor, who deemed that work was as good a therapy as any, did not forbid him to take on Tanglewood, but persuaded him to reduce his use of pain-killers and sleeping pills.

His week with the student orchestra did not go well, and he was dogged by yet more ill health. An attack of bronchitis, brought on by bad weather and poor accommodation, added to his breathing problems. Throughout his concert with the student orchestra, at which he performed Copland's Third Symphony, he was fighting for breath, although members of the audience were not aware of his suffering. He prepared the Boston Symphony for the Koussevitzky Memorial concert, but medications and lack of oxygen dulled his concentration, and he asked the assistant conductor of the orchestra to undertake Bright Sheng's orchestrated version of *Arias and Barcarolles*.

On the Sunday afternoon concert, all his family and many of his closest friends were present. Exhausted and visibly weak, Bernstein opened the programme with Britten's *Four Sea Interludes* from *Peter Grimes*, then left the stage for the performance of *Arias and Barcarolles*. After the interval, he returned to conduct Beethoven's Seventh Symphony. Scarcely moving and hardly lifting his arms, the conductor, whose acrobatic leaps and so-called 'chorybantics' had thrilled audiences and infuriated his critics, willed the orchestra to play by the sheer force of his presence. During the third movement, he suffered a coughing fit and stopped conducting altogether, holding the rail round the podium for support. The Boston musicians kept playing, following the concertmaster of the orchestra, until Bernstein could resume. In the final movement, he regained control, completing the work with a customary fire that must have sapped his remaining energy. After an appearance at the traditional post-concert reception, Bernstein returned the same evening to New York. The European tour with the students was cancelled. For weeks, he had been surviving on excessive doses of medical drugs and alcohol, and he spent his seventy-second birthday in Lenox Hill hospital undergoing a 'drying out' process. His New York apartment had also taken on the appearance of a hospital, staffed by nurses and with doctors and a psychiatrist on hand to deal with problems of drug dependency.

In September he moved to his home in Connecticut, leaving most of the professional medical staff behind, and depending on the care of friends and assistants. The news cast a ray of hope. The malignancy had gone, and the earlier treatment had cured his cancer. But serious emphysema – almost as deadly – called for the strictest attention, and he was suffering from a series of related problems that caused pain and discomfort, leaving him deeply depressed. There were drugs to relieve the pain, but they affected his mind. No longer able to concentrate, Bernstein could not read, nor could he bear to listen to music. No announcements were made to the press. He was resting, following illness, and future engagements had not yet been cancelled.

Opposite, this last formal portrait was taken during the Sapporo Festival in July 1990.

On 1 October Bernstein returned to New York for further medical tests. Fibrosis, an affliction of the lungs causing their rigidity (and thereby restricting breathing) was found. Living in his apartment at the Dakota, and still cared for by his own staff and his old friend Michael Wager, Bernstein was imprisoned, moving between a few of the rooms with the aid of a wheelchair. In almost constant pain and convinced of imminent death, he even contemplated suicide.

A more balanced diet of medicines allowed him to think more lucidly, and he made new plans. His first was to retire from conducting and, in the words of the press statement that followed, 'devote his professional energies to composing, writing and education'. It went on to list a number of compositions on which he was working, as well as educational projects, and even his memoirs. The news took everyone, including some of Bernstein's close working colleagues, by surprise. Even then, few seemed aware of the gravity of his condition.

By the second week of October, a further cancerous growth had been found, and plans were made for more hospital tests. In the meantime, close friends and family made visits whenever he felt well enough to see them. Many realized that they were moments of farewell. On the evening of 14 October, while being treated by his

doctor, Bernstein suffered a fatal heart attack 'brought on by progressive emphysema complicated by a pleural tumour and a series of pulmonary infections'.

The shocking news circulated around the world, occupying the international headlines of newspapers, radio and television in many countries. For musicians and those associated with the concert world, it was unthinkable. Leonard Bernstein had been a guiding musical light for half a century. His death also represented the departure of a well-known face and a vibrant personality that had acquired the familiarity of a favourite friend for millions of non-musicians and non-performers: television viewers, concert-goers, lovers of the theatre and the entertainment world. His was a household name synonymous with music of every kind.

There were a series of memorial services, during which his family, friends, colleagues and fellow-musicians offered eloquent and heartfelt tributes. In a much wider world, however, there was an uncounted mass of ordinary people who had never met or known him, knew nothing specific about his public or private lives, yet still felt a sense of personal loss.

In July of 1937, a teenage piano student, working as a music counsellor at Camp Onota, Massachusetts, had hushed a noisy lunch in the canteen with a loud chord on the piano. When the room was silent, he announced that George Gershwin, 'America's greatest Jewish composer', had just died. Then, with a request for no applause at the end of the piece, he played Gershwin's second Prelude for piano. The performer was, of course, Leonard Bernstein. It would be heart-warming to think that, in October of 1990, in some other place and at a different gathering, a young and as yet unknown musician made a similar declaration about the passing of another great (and even more recognizably Jewish) composer and, in his own way, played his tribute.

Epilogue

Conductor, composer, pianist, television personality, teacher and, above all, communicator, Leonard Bernstein was unquestionably the most famous classical musican of the second half of the twentieth century. He is also the most documented. All his music and writings are in print; his recordings run into hundreds; there are films of many of his major orchestral interpretations, and his television programmes are available for students and viewers to study and enjoy. In keeping with our times, there is even a Bernstein web-site on the Internet.

His musical legacy is unique. No composer has ever been as comfortably at home in the concert hall, the opera house and the Broadway theatre, and none with such success. Bernstein has been compared with George Gershwin, but the parallel is erroneous. Gershwin, one of the most original musicians of the twentieth century, introduced jazz – a unique American musical form – into the concert hall, but he could not be considered a classical composer. Even his *Porgy and Bess* (performed in the opera house) is more truly a folk opera (not unlike *The Beggar's Opera* assembled by John Gay), which presents popular music in an operatic form and is a 'serious' extension of the Broadway theatre. Kurt Weill, another composer with whom parallels have been drawn, began his career as a classical composer, but added nothing to that medium after the 1920s, devoting the rest of his creative life to politically motivated music-theatre, to film music and to traditional musical comedies.

Throughout his career, Bernstein never 'changed sides'. He developed an original musical style that is an amalgam of the musical influences – Hebrew liturgy, the classical repertoire, jazz, popular music – that were part of his life. His work in music-theatre was often pioneering. We may take *West Side Story* for granted today, but it was ground-breaking stuff in 1957, introducing racial prejudice, social injustice and unhappily true-to-life street violence into an entertainment that had previously contented itself with charming trivialities. Fourteen years later, *Mass* set out to create an ecumenical pageant-like experience that would blend classical, jazz, popular and contemporary rock music. He was always brimming with imaginative and innovative ideas, from his *Age of Anxiety* Symphony (1949), which introduces a mini jazz piano concerto, to Concerto for Orchestra (1989), which uses free-form improvisation, anagrams, mystical numbers and mathematical puzzles within the structure of the music. Almost his entire creative output developed original observations and experimented with musical techniques. At the same time, he never bowed before the musical altar of political correctness, standing firm against the demands of serialism when so many of his contemporaries felt obliged to accede to them. He had a brilliant mind, but he composed music from his heart. Many fascinating theatre projects (involving works by Brecht, Wilder and Nabokov, to name a few) were started but, frustratingly, abandoned, and one can only hope that, for historical reasons, some of the preparatory sketches may one day be made available.

Sadly, few of the serious works enjoyed unanimous critical acclaim. To his chagrin, none of them even earned the prestigious Pulitzer Prize, an honour conferred on the works of several lesser composers. In later years, Bernstein seemed increasingly obsessed with composing that one elusive masterpiece by which he would be forever remembered, but it did not happen. Perhaps he was too often distracted by the need to perform, and the instant gratification that an adoring public brought to him. As Bernstein's universal fame and popularity grew, one had the feeling that the critics were 'gunning' for him, damning each new offering with faint praise, with sullen indifference or with open hostility towards the man as much as his music. Not every new work was destined for immortality, but many of them deserved a better fate or, at least, a kinder reception. Perhaps, as the pile of uncompleted projects and negative reviews grew higher, Bernstein sought solace on the concert podium, where he knew he was always among friends. It is also possible that his self-indulgent lifestyle – too many parties, too much alcohol, too many 'uppers' and 'downers' – blunted his concentration. But his inventiveness never diminished, as the brilliant intricacies of Concerto for Orchestra prove.

Viewed from a distance, and shielded by a loving public relations machine that endeavoured to protect a somewhat tarnished personal image, Leonard Bernstein was revered and sought after by an international audience that stretched from Vienna to Tokyo and back. Musicians everywhere were grateful for the inspiration and artistic leadership with which he enriched their lives, and New Yorkers loved 'Lenny' without reservation, delighting in his extravagant persona and superstar lifestyle almost as much as his critics disapproved of it. When he died, the motorcade that carried his coffin across Manhattan was witnessed by thousands, who paused for a moment to mourn the passing of a favourite adopted son and, indeed, a great man.

It will be for future musicians, musicologists and historians to sift through everything Bernstein undertook and, with the perspective of time, to reach more concrete conclusions on his contributions to music in the twentieth century. He was a dominant and persuasive advocate of his art for more than forty years, and brought classical music to a wider audience than any predecessor. Contrary to his fears, he will be remembered as much more than just 'the man who wrote *West Side Story*'.

Classified List of Works

All first performance dates (fp) are given where available. Sung or spoken works are in English except where otherwise noted.

Stage and Screen Works

Fancy Free, ballet, choreography by Jerome Robbins (1944). fp New York, 18 April 1944

On the Town, musical, lyrics and book by Betty Comden and Adolph Green (1944). fp New York, 28 December 1944

Facsimile, ballet, choreography by Jerome Robbins (1946). fp New York, 24 October 1946

Peter Pan, incidental music, lyrics by Leonard Bernstein (1950). fp New York, 24 April 1950

Trouble in Tahiti, opera in one act, libretto by Leonard Bernstein (1952). fp Brandeis Festival, Massachusetts, 12 June 1952

Wonderful Town, musical, lyrics by Betty Comden and Adolph Green, book by Joseph A. Fields and Jerome Chodorov (1952). fp New York, 26 February, 1953

On the Waterfront, film score, director: Elia Kazan (1954)

The Lark, incidental music, text by Lillian Hellman after Jean Anouilh's play *L'Alouette* (1955). fp New York, 17 November 1955

Candide, comic operetta, lyrics by Richard Wilbur, additional lyrics by John Latouche, Dorothy Parker and Leonard Bernstein, book by Lillian Hellman, adapted from Voltaire's novella (1956). fp New York, 1 December 1956. Revised over a period of thirty years.

Candide, comic operetta, final version, lyrics by Richard Wilbur, additional lyrics by John Latouche, Dorothy Parker, Lillian Hellman, Leonard Bernstein, Stephen Sondheim and John Wells, book by Hugh Wheeler, adapted from Voltaire's novella (1988). fp Glasgow, 16 May 1988

West Side Story, musical, lyrics by Stephen Sondheim, book by Arthur Laurents, based on a conception of Jerome Robbins (1957). fp New York, 26 September 1957

Mass: A Theatre Piece for Singers, Players and Dancers, text (in Latin) from the Liturgy of the Roman Mass, additional texts by Stephen Schwartz, Leonard Bernstein and Paul Simon (1971). fp Washington DC, 8 September 1971

Dybbuk, ballet, text (in Hebrew) from *Havdalah* (Jewish Sabbath service), 1 Samuel 20:4 and The Song of Solomon 4:1 (1974). fp New York, 16 May 1974

1600 Pennsylvania Avenue, musical, lyrics and book by Alan Jay Lerner (1976). fp New York, 4 May 1976

A Quiet Place, opera in two acts, libretto by Leonard Bernstein and Stephen Wadsworth (1983). fp Houston, Texas, 19 June 1983. Revised in three acts, incorporating *Trouble in Tahiti*. fp 19 June 1984

Orchestral Works

Symphony No. 1 (*Jeremiah*), for mezzo-soprano and orchestra, text (in Hebrew) from The Lamentations of Jeremiah (1943). fp Pittsburgh, Pennsylvania, 28 January 1944

Three Dance Variations from *Fancy Free* (1946)

Three Dance Episodes from *On the Town* (1945–6). fp San Francisco, February 1946

Facsimile (Choreographic Essay), concert version of ballet (1947)

Symphony No. 2 (*The Age of Anxiety*), for piano and orchestra, after poem by W. H. Auden (1949). fp Boston, 8 April 1949; (revised version) New York, 15 July 1965

Serenade, after Plato's 'Symposium', for solo violin, strings, harp and percussion (1954). fp Venice, 12 September 1954

Prelude, Fugue and Riffs, for solo clarinet and jazz ensemble (1949). fp (TV show) 1955

Symphonic Suite from *On the Waterfront* (1955). fp Tanglewood, Massachusetts, 11 August 1955

Symphonic Dances from *West Side Story* (1961). fp New York, 13 February 1961

Symphony No. 3 (*Kaddish*), for speaker, soprano, mixed chorus, boys' choir and orchestra, text (in Aramaic and Hebrew) based on the *Kaddish* prayer, Speaker's English text by Leonard Bernstein (1961–3). fp Tel Aviv, 10 December 1963; (revised version) Mainz, 25 August 1977

Chichester Psalms, for mixed choir, boy soloist and orchestra, text (in Hebrew) from The Book of Psalms (1965). fp New York, 15 July 1965

Suites No. 1 and No. 2 from *Dybbuk*, text (in Hebrew) (1974–5). fp (separately) April 1975

Slava! A Political Overture (1977). fp Washington DC, 11 October 1977

Songfest: A Cycle of American Poems for Six Singers and Orchestra, texts in English by Frank O'Hara, Lawrence Ferlinghetti, Walt Whitman, Langston Hughes, June Jordan, Anne Bradstreet, Gertrude Stein, e. e. cummings, Conrad Aiken, Gregory Corso, Edna St Vincent Millay, Edgar Allan Poe; in Spanish by Julia de Burgos (1976–7). fp Washington DC, 11 October 1977

Three Meditations from *Mass*, for cello and orchestra (1977). fp Washington DC, 11 October 1977

Divertimento for Orchestra (1980). fp Boston, 25 September 1980

Halil ('Flute'), nocturne for solo flute, piccolo, alto flute, percussion, harp and strings (1981). fp Israel, 1981

Concerto for Orchestra, incorporating *Jubilee Games* (1985, fp 1986), *Opening Prayer* (1986) and *Variations on an Octatonic Theme* (1989), text (in Hebrew) from The Book of Numbers (1989). fp Tel Aviv, 24 April 1989

Choral Music for Church or Synagogue

Hashkiveinu, for solo tenor, mixed chorus and organ, setting of the choral prayer *Hashkiveinu* from the Sabbath service, text in Hebrew (1945)

Missa brevis, for mixed chorus and countertenor solo, or seven solo voices, with percussion and handbells, text in Latin, adapted from incidental music to *The Lark*. fp 1988

Chamber Music

Sonata for Clarinet and Piano (1942). fp New York, 14 March 1943

Brass Music, five pieces for horn, trumpet, trombone, tuba and piano (1955)

Shivaree, fanfare for double brass ensemble and percussion (1969)

Dance Suite, five pieces for brass quintet. fp New York, 14 January 1990

Vocal Music

I Hate Music: A Cycle of Five Kid Songs for Soprano and Piano, text by Leonard Bernstein (1943). fp New York, 13 November 1943

La Bonne Cuisine: Four Recipes for Voice and Piano, French text by E. Dutoit, translated by Leonard Bernstein (1948)

Two Love Songs, text by Rilke (1949)

Silhouette, text adapted from Galilee by Leonard Bernstein (1951)

Get Help!, marching song, text by Leonard Bernstein (1955)

Arias and Barcarolles, for mezzo-soprano, baritone and piano four hands, text (in English) by Leonard Bernstein and Jennie Bernstein, (in Yiddish) by Yankev-Yitskhok Segal (1988). fp New York, April 1988

A Song Album, individual songs not published elsewhere, as well as the two early cycles and songs from *Peter Pan, Candide, Mass* and *1600 Pennsylvania Avenue* (1988)

Piano

Seven Anniversaries (1944)

Four Anniversaries (1948)

Five Anniversaries (1965)

Thirteen Anniversaries (1988)

Touches: Chorale, Eight Variations and Coda (1981)

Miscellaneous

Fanfares, choruses, songs and piano pieces, which served as birthday and wedding presents and other tributes

Further Reading

Numerous biographies, portraits and essays discuss Bernstein's life and works; some are included below. Many general works offer insights into the musical worlds he dominated. Two of these are *Broadway* by B. Atkinson, the doyen of Broadway critics, published in 1974, and Harold Schonberg's *The Great Conductors*, published in 1967. Schonberg, one of New York's most distinguished music critics, took Bernstein to task for his excesses, but gave credit when and where it was due.

Writings by Leonard Bernstein

Findings, 1982 (Arlington, Texas, Anchor Books, 1993)

The Infinite Variety of Music, 1966 (Arlington, Texas, Anchor Books, 1993)

The Joy of Music, 1959 (Arlington, Texas, Anchor Books, 1994)

Leonard Bernstein's Young People's Concerts, 1962 (Arlington, Texas, Anchor Books, 1992)

The Unanswered Question, 1973 Charles Eliot Norton lectures given at Harvard University (Cambridge, Mass., Harvard University Press, 1976)

Books on Leonard Bernstein

Burton, H. *Leonard Bernstein* (London, Faber and Faber, 1994)
Engagingly written, thorough biography by a friend and colleague for thirty years. A definitive history.

Burton, W. *Conversations about Bernstein* (Oxford, Oxford University Press, 1995)
Taped interviews with fellow-composers, performers, authors and many others create a personal and at times moving portrait of a much-loved artist.

Chapin, S. *Musical Chairs: A Life in the Arts* (New York, Putnam, 1977)

Chapin, S. *Leonard Bernstein: Notes from a Friend* (New York, Walker, 1992)
From his time at Columbia Masterworks to Lincoln Center, thence to Amberson Productions and, in 1971, to the Metropolitan Opera, Chapin's life was linked with Bernstein's, as colleague and close family friend.

Fluegel, J. *Bernstein Remembered* (New York, Carroll & Graf, 1991)
A portrait accompanied by excellent photographs.

Gottlieb, J. (ed.) *Bernstein on Broadway* (New York, Amberson, 1981)
Articles by George Abbot, Harold Prince, Jerome Robbins, Stephen Sondheim, Betty Comden and Adolph Green, edited by an assistant of Bernstein's for many years.

Gruen, J. *The Private World of Leonard Bernstein* (New York, Ridge Press and Viking Press, 1968)
Published with the collaboration of the Bernstein family, and with excellent photographs by Ken Hyman, this book has been criticized for its 'coffee-table' attributes, but is an endearing family portrait from one of the happier periods in the artist's life.

Peyser, J. *Bernstein: A Biography* (London, Bantam Press, 1987)
An unattractive investigation of some of the tabloid aspects of Bernstein's private life, it nevertheless presents good background material on post-war musical developments. It includes some questionable, spec-ulative theories on Bernstein's psychological make-up.

Secrest, M. *Leonard Bernstein: A Life* (London, Bloomsbury, 1995)
Gaps in information result from the author's lack of access to the substantial Bernstein archive. Her research in some quarters met with a 'wall of silence', but this may have been triggered by reactions to the revelations in Joan Peyser's (earlier) book. It is, however, an interesting non-partisan portrait rather than a detailed biography, avoiding either condemnation or idolatry.

Selective Discography

As one of the major conductors of the second half of the twentieth century, Leonard Bernstein created one of the largest overall record catalogues in the world. His first discs were for RCA in New York, but the bulk of his recordings were made for American Columbia Records (later CBS, now Sony) and Deutsche Grammophon GmbH (DG). For the purpose of this book, I have included only recordings conducted by Bernstein himself. As the record industry makes frequent deletions and reissues, the records listed are those available at the time of going to press. (Note: a number of the works are only available as part of multi-record sets.)

Orchestral

Concerto for Orchestra ('Jubilee Games')
Israel Philharmonic Orchestra
DG 429 231-2GH

Three Meditations from Mass
Mstislav Rostropovich (cello), Israel Philharmonic Orchestra
DG 437 952-2GX2

On the Town – Three Dance Episodes
New York Philharmonic Orchestra
SONY SMK 47530

On the Waterfront – Symphonic Suite
Israel Philharmonic Orchestra
DG 415 253-2GH2

Prelude, Fugue and Riffs
Benny Goodman (clarinet), Columbia Jazz Combo
SONY SM3K 47162

Symphony No. 1 (Jeremiah)
Symphony No. 2 (The Age of Anxiety)
Symphony No. 3 (Kaddish) (revised version)
Serenade, after Plato's 'Symposium'
Christa Ludwig (mezzo-soprano, *Jeremiah*); Lukas Foss (piano, *Age of Anxiety*); Michael Wager (speaker), Montserrat Caballé (soprano), Wiener Jeunesse-Chor, Vienna Boys' Choir (*Kaddish*); Gidon Kremer (violin, *Serenade*); Israel Philharmonic Orchestra
DG 445 245-2GC2

Symphony No. 3 (Kaddish) (first version)
Felicia Montealegre (speaker), Jennie Tourel (soprano), Camerata Singers, New York Philharmonic Orchestra
SONY SM3K 47162

West Side Story – Symphonic Dances
Los Angeles Philharmonic Orchestra; with Gershwin's *Rhapsody in Blue*
DG 410 025-2GH

West Side Story – Symphonic Dances
On the Waterfront – Symphonic Suite
On the Town – Three Dance Episodes
Candide – Overture
New York Philharmonic Orchestra; with *On the Town, Facsimile, Fancy Free* and *Trouble in Tahiti* (all complete)
SONY SM3K 47154

Vocal and Choral

Chichester Psalms
Songfest
Soloist from the Vienna Boys' Choir, Wiener Jeunesse-Chor, Israel Philharmonic Orchestra (*Chichester Psalms*); Clamma Dale, Rosalind Elias, Nancy Williams, Neil Rosenshein, John Reardon, Donald Gramm, National Symphony Orchestra (*Songfest*)
DG 415 965-2GH

Stage Works

Candide (first version)
Robert Rounseville, Barbara Cook, Max Adrian, Irra
Petina, William Olvis, George Blackwell, Thomas Pyle,
Norman Roland, William Chapman, Robert
Mesrobian, Martin Beck Theatre Chorus & Orchestra
conducted by Samuel Krachmalnick
SONY SK 48017 (original cast recording, 1956)

Candide (final version, 1988)
Jerry Hadley, June Anderson, Adolph Green, Christa
Ludwig, Nicolai Gedda, Della Jones, Kurt Ollmann,
Clive Bayley, Neil Jenkins, Lindsay Benson, Richard
Suart, John Treleaven, London Symphony Chorus and
Orchestra
DG 435 487-2GH

Dybbuk (complete ballet)
New York City Ballet Orchestra
SONY SM3K 47158

Facsimile
New York Philharmonic Orchestra
SONY SM3K 47154

Fancy Free
New York Philharmonic Orchestra
SONY SM3K 47154

Mass
Alan Titus, Norman Scribner Choir, Berkshire Boy
Choir, Alvin Ailey American Dance Theatre
SONY SM2K 44593

A Quiet Place
Chester Ludgin, Beverly Morgan, John Branstetter,
Peter Kazaras, Jean Kraft, Theodor Uppman, Clarity
James, John Kuether, Charles Walker, Douglas Perry,
Wendy White, Edward Crafts, Louise Edeiken, Mark
Thomsen, Kurt Ollmann, Austrian Radio Symphony
Chorus and Orchestra
DG 439 251-2GY

West Side Story
Kiri Te Kanawa, José Carreras, Tatiana Troyanos, Kurt
Ollmann, Marilyn Horne, Louise Edeiken, Angela
Réaux, Stella Zambalis, David Livingston, Mary
Nelson, Stephen Bogardus, Peter Thom, Todd Lester,
Richard Harrell, Broadway Orchestra and Chorus
DG 415 963-2GH

Index

Page numbers in italics refer to
picture captions.

Photographic Acknowledgements

BFI Stills, London: 72–3, 87, 126–7
The Boston Symphony Orchestra,
    Boston: 70
CBS Records: 172–3
Corbis-Bettmann, London: 11, 13,
    16, 22, 43 (John Springer
    Collection), 75
Corbis-Bettmann/UPI: 60, 61, 65,
    83, 114 l+r, 140, 155, 186, 190, 193,
    211
The Curtis Institute of Music
    Library, Philadelphia: 30–1
Deutsche Grammophon GmbH:
    199 (photo Schaffler), 205 (photo
    Don Hunstein), 206 (photo
    Vienna State Opera), 208–9
(photo Henry Grossman), 212
(photo Christina Burton), 215
(photo Christina Burton), 216–7
(photo Christina Burton), 223
(photo Eiichiro Sakata)
The Frank Driggs Collection,
    New York: 68, 69
The Hulton Getty Picture
    Collection, London: 33, 129, 131,
    151, 167, 182
The Hulton Getty Picture
    Collection, London/Corbis,
    London: 49, 128, 175
The Lebrecht Collection, London:
    42, 110, 197 (© John Minnion)
The Museum of the City of New
    York, New York: 104–5
The New York Philharmonic
    Archives, New York: 85, 115, 136
New York Times Pictures, New
    York: 40
Photofest, New York: 26, 28, 39,
    46, 66–7, 80–1 (photo
    Vandamm), 97, 99, 103 (photo
    Fehl), 108, 139, 160–1, 180, 189,
    195
Popperfoto, Northampton: 51, 101,
    125, 148–9, 166
Richard Rodzinski: 54
Sony Music, New York: 2, 119, 123
    (photo Don Hunstein)
Roy Stevens: 90

Text Acknowledgement

Lines by Paul Simon quoted from
Mass © Copyright 1971, 1972 by
the Estate of Leonard Bernstein
and Stephen Schwartz.
Reprinted by permission of
Leonard Bernstein Music
Publishing Company LLC,
Publisher and Boosey & Hawkes,
Inc., Sole Agent.